gardening workbo

Spring in the Garden

gardening workbooks

Spring in the Garden

Steven Bradley

photography by **Anne Hyde**

RYLAND
PETERS
& SMALL

First published in Great Britain in 1998

by Ryland Peters & Small

Cavendish House

51–55 Mortimer Street

London W1N 7TD

Printed in China
Produced by Sun Fung Offset Binding Co., Ltd.

ISBN 1 900518 46 5

A catalogue record for this book is available from the British Library

Designer **Prue Bucknall**

Editor **Toria Leitch**

Production **Kate Mackillop**

Illustrators **Polly Raynes, Amanda Patton, Gill Tomblin, Ann Winterbotham, Lesley Craig**

contents

spring can be the most stressful period of the gardening year. Too much to do, too little time to do it, and of course the plants can't wait to get started. All those months of planning and preparation whilst waiting for the weather to change are transferred into a flurry of frenetic activity as the plans are finally put into operation. Timing is critical: how to get the earliest possible start, but at the same time beat the spring frosts. Day temperatures can soar for several hours before plunging to freezing in the early hours of the morning. Strong winds thrash young foliage and heavy rain batters tender seedlings – yet still we are glad that spring has finally arrived.

This season provides a perfect opportunity to create something new, either a short-term project, such as filling and planting a hanging basket for a summer display, or perhaps something more permanent, such as planting a climber or tree, which will provide interest and colour for many years to come.

Spring is also the perfect time of year for renovation of those shrubs which need a severe pruning to stimulate new growth, as it is far better to prune them just before the new growth starts or immediately after flowering. The lawn can look pretty sad after the ravages of winter, and spring is the ideal time for repairing damaged areas, improving surface drainage and dealing with any moss which has survived the winter. Feeding, weeding and mowing are all used to encourage rapid grass growth and restore the lawn to its former glory. Start the season by carrying out any necessary repairs on machinery and equipment before they are needed for the busy coming year in the garden.

Steven Bradley

new introductions

For most gardeners, the prospect of adding new plants to the garden is irresistible, no matter how experienced they may be. Either the aquisition of new plants or raising them from seed or cuttings for that little space in the garden will always be a source of excitement. There is a great deal of overlap in the gardening operations that are carried out between autumn and spring, with many tasks being carried out at either the beginning or the end of the growing season. Often, what will determine when tasks are performed will be the hardiness or growth patterns of the plants concerned, with more tender plants being saved until the spring when they can be planted as the weather improves, rather than overwintering them.

Planting Bulbs

'Bulb' is the generic term which is often loosely used to describe bulbous plants, such as bulbs, corms, rhizomes and tubers. These are all plants where a portion of the root is modified to form a swollen food-store, which will keep the plant alive through its dormant, or 'resting', period. Although the majority of bulbs are planted in the autumn for an early spring flowering display, some should be left until the spring – particularly those that flower in the summer and early autumn. The flowers produced by these spring-planted bulbs are often larger, more exotic and more varied in their range of colours than their spring counterparts.

Late-flowering bulbs

Summer- and autumn-flowering bulbs must have a soil which retains plenty of moisture through the summer while they are growing, but is free-draining in the winter to prevent them from rotting while they are dormant. Late-flowering bulbs are ideal for planting in mixed borders – to extend the season of interest and give the border an 'early start'. Bulbs can be selected to develop and flower before many of the shrubs and herbaceous perennials have started to flower. Another added attraction with some summer- and autumn-flowering bulbs is that the seed heads may be kept after the blooms are finished, for instance, ornamental onions (*Alliums*) are particularly valuable for this purpose. The old seed heads can either be left *in situ* where they will last well into the winter, or be cut and hung to dry before being used in dried flower arrangements.

Alstroemeria

Lilium candidum

Lilium *'Enchantment'*

Summer- and autumn-flowering bulbs

- Arum lily (*Zantedeschia aethiopica*)
- *Crocosmia*
- Foxtail lily (*Eremurus*)
- Giant lily (*Cardiocrinum*)
- Gladiolus
- Lily (*Lilium*)
- Onion (*Allium*)
- Peruvian lily (*Alstroemeria*)
- *Schizostylis coccinea*
- Sorrel (*Oxalis*)

Preparing for planting

Bulbs which grow and flower later in the year frequently have to endure some of the driest growing conditions and will often root quite deeply into the soil to find moisture. Incorporating generous quantities of well-rotted organic matter before planting will aid moisture retention. Bulbs are normally sold and planted while they are dry, with no roots or leaves. However, snowdrops (*Galanthus*) will establish better if transplanted almost immediately after flowering 'in the green' (see right) with the leaves still present, when new roots are produced very quickly.

How deep to plant

If planted too shallowly, bulbs can push themselves out of the ground as the new roots develop in the spring, and in these conditions they will not produce flowers. Planting depth is usually determined by the size of bulb being planted. Two to three times the length of the bulb is the usual planting depth, but one or two of the summer- and autumn-flowering bulbs, such as *Crinum* and *Nerine*, are planted with their tips at soil level. With groups, allow three or four bulb widths apart, so that strong stems can develop to hold up the flowers.

Planting in the ground

1 Dig a planting hole large enough to accommodate your bulbs. Use a trowel for small bulbs, or a spade for larger ones or where you are planting a large group.

2 Break up the soil in the bottom of the hole with a trowel or hand fork and place each bulb into the hole in an upright position, and press them into the soil.

3 Using the trowel, pull the soil back into the hole, covering the bulb to the right depth. Firm gently into place and water.

Planting in baskets

Any type of bulb can be planted in a wire or plastic basket. This is a clever device to use if you wish to move your plants, for instance, once the foliage has died off in preparation for lifting, dividing and storing, or for tender bulbs that need to be put indoors over winter.

1 Line the bottom of the basket with enough soil so that the bulbs will be planted at their correct depth. Then position the bulbs you have chosen on top of the layer of soil, spacing them out evenly.

2 Fill the basket with soil and lower it into a hole, deep enough so that the top rim sits just below soil level. Cover the top of the basket with soil and mark its position.

3 After planting, cover the area with a mulch of sharp gravel – this will deter slugs and snails from eating the shoots as they emerge, as they do not like travelling across sharp surfaces, and applying such a barrier also reduces the need to use chemical baits.

Planting Perennials

The majority of perennials are planted in the autumn, when the soil is still warm and they are able to get established for a quick start in the spring. However, more tender plants should be saved until spring, when they can be planted as the weather improves, rather than taking the risk of overwintering them.

Tender perennials

Certain plants should only be considered for planting in the spring, as they will not survive if left in cold and wet winter conditions. These include plants with hollow stems or hairy leaves, which usually have silver or grey foliage. Those plants with hollow stems are very susceptible to rainwater being trapped within the stem, which may lead to the stems rotting at the base and the rot spreading into the remainder of the plant. Plants which have a hairy coating on the leaves (and often the stems) can trap water between the hairs on the surface of the leaves, which can also lead to damage through rotting.

Papaver orientale

Phlox maculata *'Omaga'*

Delphiniums

Plants with hollow stems	**Season of interest**	**Height**
Alcanet (*Anchusa*)	summer	50 cm (20 in)
Blazing star (*Liatris*)	summer	1.2 m (4 ft)
Comfrey (*Symphytum*)	spring	25–50 cm (10–20 in)
Delphinium	summer	1–1.8 m (3–6 ft)
Ligularia	summer	1.2 m (4 ft)
Nerine	autumn	60 cm (2 ft)
Phlox	summer	10–30 cm (4–12 in)
Poppy (*Papaver*)	summer	20–45 cm (8–18 in)
Red hot poker (*Kniphofia*)	summer	1–1.8 m (3–6 ft)
Spurge (*Euphorbia*)	summer	2–4 m (6–12 ft)
Stonecrop (*Sedum*)	summer	5–20 cm (2–8 in)
Sunflower (*Helianthus*)	summer	1–3 m (3–10 ft)
Plants with hairy foliage		
Aster amellus	summer	50 cm (20 in)
Blanket flower (*Gaillardia*)	summer	45–60 cm (18–24 in)
Brunnera	spring	45 cm (18 in)
Campion (*Lychnis*)	summer	15–30 cm (6–12 in)
Catmint (*Nepeta*)	summer	40–80 cm (16–32 in)
Cupid's dart (*Catananche*)	summer	45–60 cm (18–24 in)
Hedge nettle (*Stachys*)	spring/summer	15–45 cm (6–18 in)
Lungwort (*Pulmonaria*)	spring	25 cm (10 in)
Pearl everlasting (*Anaphalis*)	late summer	60 cm (2 ft)
Pincushion flower (*Scabiosa*)	spring/summer	30–90 cm (1–3 ft)
Tanacetum syn. *Pyrethrum*	summer	30–75 cm (12–30 in)

Preparing the soil and planting perennials

Herbaceous perennials will usually occupy the same site for at least three years, so the soil must be well cultivated before planting. Test the pH and adjust it, if necessary, to aim for a level of between 6.5 and 7.0, which will suit most plants. Increase acidity (lowering the pH) by adding peat, or raise the alkaline content by applying a dressing of lime.

Planting depths

1 Plants with a fibrous root system should have the topmost root about 1 cm (½ in) below soil level.

2 Those with a thick fleshy root, or a cluster or crown of buds should be around 2.5 cm (1 in) below soil level.

3 In soils that are prone to waterlogging the base should be planted slightly proud of the soil level to avoid rotting.

Planting perennials

Perennials can be bought either as bare-rooted plants or container-grown. In heavy (clay) soils, it is wiser to use bare-rooted plants, as water from the surrounding clay soil tends to seep into the planting hole and will cause waterlogging around the root ball.

1 Dig a planting hole that is large enough to comfortably accommodate the whole root system. Hold the plant by its stem or leaves to avoid damaging the roots (if your plant is container-grown remove it from its pot first) and place it carefully into the hole.

2 Using a trowel, fill the hole with soil around the plant and firm in, leaving a slight depression around the stem.

3 Water the plant in around the base with enough water to thoroughly settle the roots, filling the depression made earlier.

4 Once they have started to grow, some of the taller plants will need supporting with twigs to prevent them falling over. Tie the stems to the supports with garden twine. As they grow taller the plants will fill out and disguise their twiggy framework.

Planting Annuals and Biennials

The spring season provides a perfect opportunity to create a short-term bedding display which provides splashes of foliage and colour in spaces that will eventually be filled by more permanent plantings. Interest can also be provided by sowing patches of annual grasses into the border between other plants. The gentle swaying movement and rustling of seed heads add an extra dimension.

Seed sown outdoors

The easiest way to grow annuals and biennials is to sow them directly into the ground outside, at the beginning of spring when the soil is starting to warm up again. For instructions on planting annual seeds outdoors, see page 36.

Dianthus barbatus

Lavatera trimestris

Lunaria annua

Annuals and biennials for spring sowing	Season of interest	Height
Baby's breath (*Gypsophila paniculata*)	summer	1.2 m (4 ft)
Black-eyed Susan (*Rudbeckia hirta*)	summer	30–90 cm (1–3 ft)
Canterbury bells (*Campanula medium*)	spring/summer	60–90 cm (2–3 ft)
Gillyflower (*Matthiola incana*)	summer	80 cm (32 in)
Hollyhock (*Alcea ficifolia*)	summer	2.5 m (8 ft)
Honesty (*Lunaria annua*)	spring/summer	75 cm (30 in)
Love-in-a-mist (*Nigella*)	summer	45–75 cm (18–30 in)
Mallow (*Lavatera trimestris*)	summer	1.2 m (4 ft)
Marigold (*Calendula officinalis*)	summer	30–70 cm (12–28 in)
Sweet William (*Dianthus barbatus*)	summer	70 cm (28 in)
Annual and biennial grasses for spring sowing		
Fountain grass (*Pennisetum setaceum*)	summer	1 m (3 ft)
Greater quaking grass (*Briza maxima*)	summer	50 cm (20 in)
Hare's tail (*Lagurus ovatus*)	summer	45 cm (18 in)
Job's tears (*Coix lacryma-jobi*)	autumn	45–90 cm (18–36 in)
Maize (*Zea mays*)	summer	90–120 cm (3–4 ft)
Squirrel tail grass (*Hordeum jubatum*)	summer	30 cm (1 ft)
Switch grass (*Panicum virgatum*)	autumn	1 m (3 ft)

Seed sown indoors

In order to extend the flowering season even further, some hardy annuals can be raised early by sowing them under protection in a greenhouse or cold frame, and planting them out as young plants. See page 38 for 'Sowing Seeds Indoors'. Once they have grown to a suitable size, they can be planted out as a clump or group in the border.

Planting Herbs

These aromatic plants, usually associated with culinary skills and food seasoning, also include a number of attractive ornamental garden plants which may be grown for their looks. Almost all herbs prefer to grow in a sunny position with a fertile, free-draining compost. The site must be cultivated deeply and cleared of all perennial weeds before any planting can be considered.

A culinary herb border

Traditionally, herb beds are arranged in a formal design to define the individual herbs and prevent plants becoming too straggly. Shrubby herbs are used as a framework planting to provide focal points and boundaries, into which the annual and biennial herbs are used as groundwork or filling. A modern approach is to lay out the paths in a symmetrical pattern to create beds, but soften this effect with informal plantings within the beds, which will provide colour, aroma, leaf texture and variations in height and shape.

Use the plan above and the chart below as a guide to planting your herbs and see pages 11–13 for planting techniques.

	Common herbs	Season of interest	Height
A	Mint (*Mentha spicata*)	summer	30–90 cm (1–3 ft)
B	Borage (*Borago officinalis*)	summer	30–90 cm (1–3 ft)
C	Basil (*Ocimum basilicum*)	summer	15–45 cm (6–18 in)
D	Parsley (*Petroselinum crispum*)	summer	30–80 cm (12–32 in)
E	Fennel (*Foeniculum vulgare*)	summer	1.8 m (6 ft)
F	Coriander (*Coriandrum sativum*)	summer	50 cm (20 in)
G	Chives (*Allium schoenoprasum*)	summer	30–60 cm (1–2 ft)
H	Thyme (*Thymus vulgaris*)	summer	15–23 cm (6–9 in)
I	Lavender (*Lavandula angustifolia*)	summer	30–60 cm (1–2 ft)
J	Sage (*Salvia officinalis*)	summer	60–80 cm (24–32 in)
K	Bay (*Laurus nobilis*)	spring/summer	3–15 m (10–50 ft)
L	Rosemary (*Rosmarinus officinalis*)	spring	1.5 m (5 ft)
M	Dill (*Anethum graveolens*)	summer	60–90 cm (2–3 ft)
N	Horseradish (*Armoracia rusticana*)	summer	30–120 cm (1–4 ft)
O	Angelica (*Angelica archangelica*)	summer	1–2.5 m (3–8 ft)

Harvesting herbs

Harvest and dry your herbs to preserve their aromatic properties. Never wash them before drying, as they may start to rot. Tie short stems into bunches of eight to ten and hang them up in a warm, dry and well-aired room until the leaves become crisp. Once dry, store the leaves in an airtight container.

Spring harvesting herbs

Angelica	Lovage
Bay	Mint
Dill	Rosemary
Fennel	Sage
Horseradish	Thyme

Planting Trees and Shrubs

Most trees and shrubs are planted in the autumn when the ground is warm. However, certain types of plants should only be considered for planting in the spring, after the risk of severe frost has diminished. These include plants with hollow stems, which are susceptible to splitting when they are exposed to low temperatures, or those with thick, fleshy leaves, which are very easily damaged by frost.

Trees which may be damaged by spring frosts	**Shrubs which may be damaged by spring frosts**
Cape wattle (*Albizia distachya*)	*Buddleja crispa*
Empress tree (*Paulownia tomentosa*)	*Carpentaria*
Honey locust (*Gleditsia triacanthos* 'Sunburst')	Chusan palm (*Trachycarpus fortunei*)
Indian bean tree (*Catalpa bignonioides* 'Aurea')	*Desfontainia spinosa*
Japanese pagoda tree (*Sophora japonica*)	New Zealand tea-tree (*Leptospermum scoparium*)
Japanese snowbell (*Styrax japonicus*)	Pineapple guava (*Acca sellowiana*)
Kalopanax pictus	Sage (*Salvia microphylla*)
Paper-bark maple (*Acer griseum*)	Shrubby germander (*Teucrium fruticans*)
Peach (*Prunus persica*)	Trailing abutilon (*Abutilon megapotamicum*)
Silver wattle (*Acacia retinodes*)	*Zenobia pulverulenta*

Planting a tree or shrub in the ground

Trees and shrubs can be bought bare-rooted, container-grown or root-balled. However, bare-root plants prefer to be planted in the autumn when it is less dry. The methods for planting are similar for all types, the main differences being that root-balled plants need a larger planting hole and bare-root plants may need their roots trimming first.

Planting a container-grown shrub

1 Mark out the area for your planting hole, about twice the width of the diameter of the root ball. Dig the hole so that it is large enough to take the entire root system and break up the sides with a garden fork to allow the roots to spread.

2 Remove the plant from its container or wrapping and loosen any tangled roots with your fingers.

3 Now place the plant carefully in the hole. For tall plants or those with smaller root balls, it is advisable to stake the plant as the roots are developing in order to anchor it securely. Place the stake next to the root ball in the planting hole, making sure that it does not damage any of the roots, and then knock it firmly into place.

4 Rest a bamboo cane across the hole to check that the top of the root ball is on the same level as the surrounding soil and then fill in the hole with soil.

5 Finally, firm the soil and water the plant thoroughly. If you are supporting the shrub with a stake, attach the stem of the plant to the stake with a strap tie and spacer.

Planting a shrub in a container

Growing trees or shrubs in containers is an excellent way of protecting tender species which may need to be brought inside over winter. It also provides the opportunity to plant trees in gardens with no soil, such as patio or roof gardens. Containers are also useful for plants which could not be grown in the garden due to the soil being unsuitable. Rhododendrons and *Magnolia campbellii*, for instance, need acidic soil conditions.

1 Make sure the container has drainage holes and place a layer of pot shards over them to stop the compost being washed out. Add a layer of compost to cover them.

2 Take two pieces of 3 x 3 cm (1½ x 1½ in) wood, and bind them together to make a small cross. Wedge it horizontally into the pot, above the compost. Insert a stake and fasten it to the cross with strong wire.

3 Place the tree in the container, spreading the roots out evenly over the compost. Then add compost around the roots and shake the stem of the tree to settle the compost.

4 Fill the container with layers of compost and firm each layer until the compost reaches up to 10 cm (4 in) below the top rim.

5 Make another larger cross out of wood and wedge it horizontally into the sides of the container, level with the compost. Fasten the stake to this cross with strong wire and cover with compost to hide the wood.

6 Fix the tree to the stake using a strap tie and spacer to prevent the stake damaging the stem. The strap tie should be about 15 cm (6 in) above the top of the container.

7 Using a saw, cut off any surplus stake about 5 cm (2 in) above the tie – use only a short stake as this allows the roots to develop whilst allowing the stem to flex and bend in the wind and reduces the chance of the container blowing over in the wind.

8 Water the compost and apply a reflective mulch of light coloured stones or wood chips to prevent the compost from drying out.

Planting Climbers

Apart from climbing roses, most climbers are purchased as container-grown plants. They can be planted at almost any time of the year, but planting in the spring offers a number of benefits: the soil is moist and starting to warm up as the days become longer and the sun warmer, providing the longest possible growing period in the new site and allowing plenty of time for the plant to establish successfully. Also, the risk of frost is diminishing, which is particularly important for plants that may not be fully hardy in your locality.

Tropaeolum speciosum

Climbers for acid soil

Agapetes serpens
Asteranthera ovata
Chilean bellflower (*Lapageria rosea*)
Coral plant (*Berberidopsis corallina*)
Dusky coral pea (*Kennedia rubicunda*)
Flame nasturtium (*Tropaeolum speciosum*)
Herald's trumpet (*Beaumontia grandiflora*)
Holboellia coriacea
Lardizabala biternata
Mitraria coccinea
Mutisia oligodon

Passiflora caerulea

Climbers for alkaline soil

Actinidia kolomikta
American bittersweet (*Celastrus scandens*)
Blue passion flower (*Passiflora caerulea*)
Campsis x *tagliabuana* 'Mme Galen'
Clematis heracleifolia
Chinese wisteria (*Wisteria sinensis*)
Chocolate vine (*Akebia quinata*)
Confederate jasmine (*Trachelospermum jasminoides*)
Everlasting pea (*Lathyrus grandiflorus*)

Humulus lupulus *'Aureus'*

Climbers for clay soil

Boston ivy (*Parthenocissus tricuspidata*)
Chinese wisteria (*Wisteria sinensis*)
Clematis (Large flowered hybrids)
Common hop (*Humulus lupulus* 'Aureus')
Common trumpet creeper (*Campsis radicans*)
Dutchman's pipe (*Aristolochia durior*)
Everlasting pea (*Lathyrus latifolius* 'White Pearl')
Virginia creeper (*Parthenocissus*)

Ipomoea

Climbers for sandy soil

Coral plant (*Berberidopsis corallina*)
Dusky coral pea (*Kennedia rubicunda*)
Flame nasturtium (*Tropaeolum speciosum*)
Giant granadilla (*Passiflora quadrangularis*)
Glory pea (*Clianthus puniceus*)
Holboellia coriacea
Ipomoea
Merremia tuberosa
Mutisia oligodon
Paradise flower (*Solanum wendlandii*)
Vitis vinifera 'Purpurea'

Planting a container-grown climber

1 Dig a planting hole large enough to accommodate the plant's root system, about 30–45 cm (1–1½ ft) away from the base of the support. Break up the soil in the base of the hole to encourage deep root penetration from the new plant.

2 Before planting, water the container thoroughly to moisten the plant's roots. Then holding the plant by its stem or leaves, gently remove it from the container and scrape away the top 1 cm (½ in) of compost from the surface of the root ball and discard it (this layer will contain most weed seeds and moss, which may contaminate the planting site).

3 Tease out any roots which are curling around the bottom of the root ball and place the plant in the hole, leaning the top of the plant against the support.

4 Mix a dressing of slow-release fertilizer into the soil which will be used to refill the planting hole. Using a spade, pull the soil back into the hole around the plant and firm it gently into place. Cover the surface of the compost with soil, leaving a slight depression around the base of the stem.

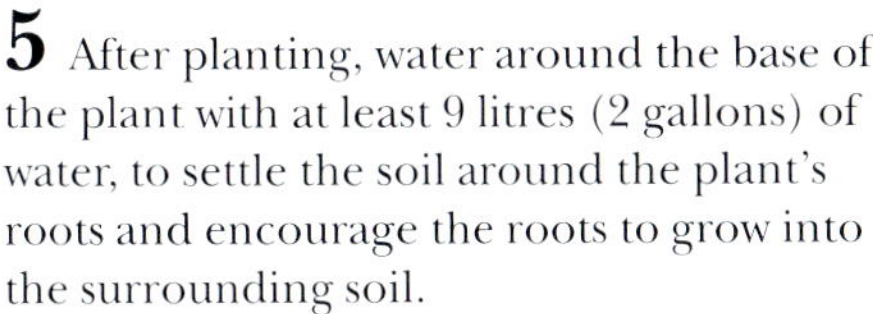

5 After planting, water around the base of the plant with at least 9 litres (2 gallons) of water, to settle the soil around the plant's roots and encourage the roots to grow into the surrounding soil.

6 Untie the shoots from the cane, spread them out against the support frame and re-tie them into position (even climbers with tendrils will need some help and guidance to start climbing in the right direction). Finally, cut out or reduce any surplus, weak or badly damaged shoots.

Routine care

Climbers are usually planted close to a wall and they may lose a lot of moisture to the wall's foundations, so it is essential to replace this loss, especially after planting. Mulching is a useful method of reducing surface evaporation from the soil, particularly with clematis, which prefers a cool, moist root system. Scatter it evenly around the root area at the base of the plant.

It is especially important to ensure that newly planted climbers are well watered. To help keep them supplied with water, a useful tip is to plant a section of plastic pipe close to the root system when the climber is planted. This pipe can be filled with water at regular intervals and the water from the pipe will then seep out into the surrounding soil, encouraging deeper rooting.

Planting Vegetables and Fruit

Spring is a time of intense activity in the vegetable garden, and this is when the bulk of the salad crops are planted, as well as alpine strawberries, ready for eating once the weather has warmed up. However, as with any other time of the year, we see both ends of the cropping cycle in spring, with seeds being sown and plants raised, as well as harvesting of some overwintered crops. Cabbages and kale are among the vegetables which can be harvested fresh and eaten.

Crop rotation

For larger gardens it is a good idea to follow a crop rotation plan in your vegetable garden: this is a system used to move vegetable crops from one plot to another on a regular basis over a number of years, reducing the effect of both pests and disease, and balancing the nutrients which are taken from the soil. Simply divide the area to be planted into four separate plots, so that each one represents one of the rotational groups, then rotate the plots from year to year.

Roots and salad crops
Carrot
Celery
Potato
Tomato

Brassicas
Cabbage
Cauliflower
Radish
Swede
Turnip

Legumes
Broad bean
French bean
Runner bean

Onions
Bulb onion
Garlic
Leek
Salad onion
Shallot

Bed systems

Where space is limited, a bed system can be used. This is a multi-row system where plants are grown close together and the distance between the rows is the same as the distance between the plants. The pathways between the beds are slightly wider than those on the row system, but because of the closer plant spacing more plants are grown. This arrangement makes the growth and shape of the vegetables more uniform. Weed control is made easier with the close spacing making the competition too fierce for the weeds to establish themselves, and the soil structure is kept in a better condition, as there is far less soil compaction.

Planting potatoes

Seed potatoes are easy to grow and need to be planted in the spring, in a frost-free environment, once the temperature has increased. The sprouts on the seed potatoes should be at least 2 cm (¾ in) long for a high yielding crop.

Varieties
'Ailsa'
'King Edward'
'Pink Fir Apple'
'Romano'
'Sante'

Prepare your soil by digging in plenty of organic matter. Dig drills or holes about 7.5–15 cm (3–6 in) deep and plant the seed potatoes about 38 cm (15 in) apart.

Cover them with 2.5 cm (1 in) of soil. In cooler climates, place a black plastic mulch over them, making holes in the cover for the emerging plants.

Planting asparagus

Asparagus is a perennial and should not be planted with your other rotational crops – set aside a separate bed. Asparagus can be sown from seed in the spring, but it is easier to buy 'crowns'. Dig 30 cm (12 in) wide trenches, 20 cm (8 in) deep and set the crowns 38 cm (15 in) apart. Cover the roots with 2.5 cm (1 in) of soil at first, adding more as the plants grow, until you reach the level of the surrounding soil.

Planting alpine strawberries

There are several different types of strawberries available and they can be broken up into three categories – summer-fruiting, perpetual-fruiting and alpine. The first two types should be planted in late summer to produce crops the following summer. However, small, sweet tasting alpine strawberries should be started in the spring.

Varieties
'Alpine Yellow'
'Baron Solemacher'
'Delicious'

Begin by sowing the seeds into trays of moist compost indoors, in early spring. Store the trays in a darkened room to aid germination (see pages 37–39 for information on sowing seeds indoors and transplanting).

After the last spring frost has passed, transplant the seedlings into beds outside. Top dress them with compost. They should produce fruit in the autumn of the first season, or failing that, the following spring.

Seeds sown outdoors

The vast majority of vegetables can be sown directly into well-prepared beds, using either a broadcast action or by sowing in drills. For instructions on sowing broadcast and in drills, see pages 36–37 in 'Propagation'.

After sowing, the seedlings are thinned out to the appropriate spacing when the first true leaf has developed. They may also need to be transplanted to permanent beds (see page 37 for instructions).

Seeds sown	Row spacing	Plant spacing
Beetroot	30 cm (12 in)	10 cm (4 in)
Broad bean	30 cm (12 in)	23 cm (9 in)
Cabbage – summer/autumn	45 cm (18 in)	30 cm (12 in)
Cabbage – winter	45 cm (18 in)	45 cm (18 in)
Calabrese	35 cm (14 in)	30 cm (12 in)
Carrot	15 cm (6 in)	10 cm (4 in)
Cauliflower – early autumn	30 cm (12 in)	15 cm (6 in)
Cauliflower – autumn	30 cm (12 in)	15 cm (6 in)
Cauliflower – winter	30 cm (12 in)	15 cm (6 in)
Cauliflower – spring	30 cm (12 in)	15 cm (6 in)
French bean	30 cm (12 in)	7.5 cm (3 in)
Kale	60 cm (24 in)	45 cm (18 in)
Kidney bean	30 cm (12 in)	15 cm (6 in)
Kohlrabi	30 cm (12 in)	15 cm (6 in)
Leek	10 cm (4 in)	2.5 cm (1 in)
Lettuce	30 cm (12 in)	30 cm (12 in)
Onion – salad	10 cm (4 in)	5 cm (2 in)
Onion – seed	30 cm (12 in)	10 cm (4 in)
Parsnip	30 cm (12 in)	15 cm (6 in)
Pea	12.5 cm (5 in)	12.5 cm (5 in)
Radish	15 cm (6 in)	2.5 cm (1 in)
Swede	38 cm (15 in)	23 cm (9 in)
Turnip	30 cm (12 in)	15 cm (6 in)

Supporting vegetables

French beans will need a support system on which to climb. Use 2.5 m (8 ft) canes and erect them in two rows, at intervals of 60 cm (2 ft), then join opposite canes together at the top and place a horizontal bar over them. The seeds are sown at the base of each cane.

Peas will also need some method of support, though not immediately. Once the seedlings have emerged plant pea sticks or twigs in the ground, either side of the drills. As the peas grow, they will attach themselves with tendrils to the sticks and gradually climb up them.

Some broad beans do not need supporting, however, taller varieties grow better if some support system is in place. Insert canes at each end of the drills, on either side of them, and attach string between them at a height of about 60 cm (2 ft), enclosing the plants.

Seeds sown indoors

Some seeds need to be started off under protection, as the soil will still be too cold for them to germinate outdoors and they risk being damaged by late spring frosts. Plant seeds in seed trays or pots (see 'Sowing Seeds Indoors', on page 38) and then put them through a gradual process of acclimatization or 'hardening-off' before you begin planting out into final positions.

Seeds sown indoors in spring

Aubergine	1 seed per 7.5 cm (3 in) pot
Broccoli	40 seeds per tray
Brussels sprouts	40 seeds per tray
Cauliflower – summer	40 seeds per tray
Celeriac	40 seeds per tray
Celery	40 seeds per tray
Cucumber	1 seed per 7.5 cm (3 in) pot
Marrow	1 seed per 7.5 cm (3 in) pot
Pepper	1 seed per 7.5 cm (3 in) pot
Sweet corn	1 seed per 7.5 cm (3 in) pot
Tomato	1 seed per 7.5 cm (3 in) pot

Hardening-off

Plants raised under cover must go through a period of acclimatization for up to two weeks before transplanting. Move them from the house or greenhouse into a cold frame or under cloches and ventilate for a few hours each day, increasing the period until the frame is left open all day. Alternatively, bring them out from the greenhouse for a couple of hours each day, then for longer periods.

Thinning and transplanting seedlings

Transplanting in spring

Plant	Row spacing	Plant spacing
Cauliflower – early summer	45 cm (18 in)	60 cm (24 in)
Cauliflower – summer	45 cm (18 in)	60 cm (24 in)
Celery	45 cm (18 in)	45 cm (18 in)
Garlic	20 cm (8 in)	20 cm (8 in)
Onion – sets	20 cm (8 in)	15 cm (6 in)
Potato	50 cm (20 in)	30 cm (12 in)

Most seedlings will need to be thinned out after they germinate to provide room for growth. If they need to be transplanted, do this when they are young, as they are better able to recover at this early stage. (See page 37 for 'Thinning seedlings' and 'Transplanting'.)

Harvesting vegetables

Some vegetables that were sown in the autumn will be ready for harvesting in spring. These include the ones in the table below. They can all be dug up out of the plot and either used immediately when they are fresh or stored for later use. Most brassicas freeze well and cabbages can be stored on a bed of straw undercover, either in a cold frame, or, if you do not have one, a garden shed will provide the necessary cover.

Spring harvesting vegetables

Broccoli	Cauliflower – winter
Brussels sprouts	Kale
Cabbage – spring	Spinach

Caring for New Plants

The most important task to consider when caring for new plants is careful planning to conserve water, which helps the new plants to grow well in dry conditions. Incorporating well-rotted organic matter into the soil increases the moisture-holding capacity of the soil, and mulching to cover the soil surface with a layer of material is an ideal way of preventing surface evaporation from the soil. It is also vital that you keep an eye on the health of the plant, dealing with any pests or diseases at an early stage, before they can do any serious damage.

Pests and diseases

Young plants and seedlings are particularly susceptible to pests and diseases so you need to give them as much protection as possible in the early stages of growth. Healthy plants are better able to cope with invasion by pests and diseases, so the first stage in preventing lasting damage is to take the best possible care of your new plants. Always use clean containers and make sure that you choose a suitable planting site with sufficient spacing; the circulation of air helps growth and the health of the plant, as well as stopping the spread of pests and diseases from one plant to another. Also, water, prune and remove any suspect leaves or branches as soon as they appear, before diseases can spread.

Diseases
The most common diseases are fungal, followed by bacterial. The most usual symptoms are discolouration and wilting or drying out of foliage and stems. Use either natural organic remedies or chemical controls to treat these problems.

Pests
On new plants the best method of control is simply to pick off the offending pests, such as slugs, snails, beetles and caterpillars. Larger four-legged pests can be deterred by a chicken wire covering placed over your plants (see right).

Watering seedlings

For seeds and seedlings, water must be in plentiful supply to enable germination and rapid development to take place. A moist seedbed is the best way to ensure that seeds will germinate quickly. If you water after sowing, the upper soil may dry out on a hot day, forming a thin crust which can prevent the seedlings emerging after germination.

Young plants being transplanted often suffer from shock and stress due to the disturbance and this is even worse in dry soil. When watering seedlings, use a light spray only; first check that your water flow is steady (see below left) and then pass the watering can gently over the plants to settle the moist soil around the roots (see below right).

Competition

Any newly planted areas need all the help they can get to establish quickly; as well as feeding and watering these new plants you also need to make sure that they do not have to compete with weeds for supplies of food and water. Some form of weed control will need to be planned and implemented therefore, to reduce this competition. Chemicals which are usually sprayed onto the weeds can be used, but the best method is to tackle weeds by hand. For the most efficient weed elimination, use a hoe. The blade should penetrate no deeper than 1 cm (½ in) into the ground, to reduce the loss of moisture from the soil and minimize soil disturbance, which encourages more weed seeds to germinate.

When hoeing out weeds between plants, sever the weeds at just below soil level, leaving the plants intact.

Mulching

A mulch is basically a covering over the soil. As well as retaining soil moisture, mulching also helps to suppress weeds. Problems can arise however, depending on the type of material being used. Straw tends to harbour insects, such as vine weevil and flea beetles, as well as contain weed seeds. If you do use an organic

mulch, make sure that it is at least 10 cm (4 in) deep in order to be effective. A good alternative is to use a black plastic film mulch, which not only warms the soil (essential at the beginning of spring) but also is easy to apply and remove. As the plants grow, you can cut a cross in the plastic and feed through the new foliage.

Shelter

Until they have established, many new plants benefit from shade and shelter to reduce water loss. To some extent these problems can be overcome by toughening the plants before they are planted out into the garden, but some form of protection for a few days can make a considerable difference to how quickly the plants start growing.

Polythene tunnels
These temporary structures are cheap, easily moved and very versatile crop covers, which can be laid over the crop (see above) and are ideal for vegetables that are grown in rows.

Fleece
For ornamental plants growing in beds, cut fleece into sheets or squares as an effective frost protector and shade-giving cover. Fleece is more permeable to light and air than plastic film.

Plastic netting
This finely-meshed material can be placed directly over seedlings or plants and anchored with pegs (see above). It is good for filtering the wind and providing overall protection.

hanging baskets

Containers filled with plants are one of the most effective methods of linking the house and garden together. They brighten up a dull corner or provide interest on a plain boring expanse of wall, adding colour for a large part of the year. The project features a classic planting plan with a large fuchsia in the centre, surrounded by smaller plants, however, you can use fewer varieties of plants in looser formation, as seen in the arrangement of impatiens, petunias, verbenas and lobelias below, or the natural looking display of nasturtiums, lobelias and helichrysums on page 29.

materials & equipment

40 cm (16 in) diameter wirework basket, rust-proofed and with a chain

wall bracket and screws

peat- or fibre-based lightweight compost

sphagnum moss

9 blue trailing lobelias (L. erinus)

1 large trailing fuchsia (F. *'Tom West'*)

3 swan river daisies (Brachyscome iberidifolia)

3 white impatiens (I. *New Guinea Group*)

3 begonias

constructing a rock garden

Rock gardens provide a very unique growing environment for a wide range of interesting and beautiful plants and they can be the ideal solution to an awkward slope where mowing or other forms of management and cultivation are difficult. They are composed of rocks and free-draining soil arranged and built to imitate a natural rocky outcrop, with plants arranged and planted between the rocks.

materials & equipment

sandstone, limestone or granite rocks

spade, rake and trowel

coarse rubble and stones

protective gloves

crowbar or strong rope

rock cress (Arabis), *trumpet gentian* (Gentiana acaulis), *pasque flower* (Pulsatilla vulgaris), Oxalis adenophylla, *moss phlox* (Phlox subulata), *meadow saxifrage* (Saxifrage granulata), Sedum spathulifolium *'Cape Blanco'*, Primula *'Blossom'*, Primula vulgaris, Lewisia tweedyi, *yarrow* (Achillea)

coarse grit mulch

propagation

Propagation is the term used to describe the deliberate multiplication of plants. For the majority of plants, spring is the beginning of the growing year and many seeds are germinated at this time, provided they are given the right environment. It is important to observe plant growth and think in terms of 'plant' time rather than simply following the calendar, because of seasonal variations and climatic changes. There are two distinct categories of propagation: sexual propagation, where many plant variations can occur and new plants originate from either seed or spores; and vegetative propagation, where new plants are clones of the original plant, and are taken from cuttings, division, grafting or layering.

Sowing Seeds Outdoors

The growth rate and habit of your plants are important in determining the spacing of the seeds, for instance, low-growing plants with a spreading habit need more space than those with an erect habit. Also, sowing too thickly produces thin, weak seedlings, and sowing too thinly wastes space. Self-seeding plants need extra room, as the seed usually disperses over a wider area than the original plants.

Sowing in drills

Sowing in drills is most commonly used for vegetables and plants that are to be grown in nursery rows and transplanted later into permanent positions. Drills are also used for plants which are sown quite close together initially but are given extra space later by thinning out the seedlings when they are large enough to handle.

Sowing broadcast

Some salad vegetables, such as radishes and salad onions, and most hardy annuals, are broadcast-sown by scattering the seed evenly onto a prepared seedbed.

This technique is most commonly used when the seedlings are intended to grow and mature *in situ* and is useful for creating a random planting effect.

1 Decide on the sowing rate per square metre (yard), according to the size and habit of the individual plant. Then on a prepared seedbed, rake the soil to establish a fine tilth.

2 Sow the seed by hand, and if the seeds are small, choose a calm day so that the wind does not blow them away. Work just above soil level so that the seed does not bounce as it lands.

3 Firm the seed gently into the seedbed with a flat board (make sure the board is dry as seeds will stick to a damp board).

4 When the bed is evenly firmed, cover the seeded area with a layer of coarse grit to a depth of at least 1 cm (½ in).

5 Using the back of a garden rake, level the grit over the seedbed. The large, coarse particles of grit allow light through to the seed, discourage slugs and suppress weed seed germination. It also absorbs the impact of rain droplets, preventing compaction and capping.

6 Finally, water the seedbed thoroughly to aid germination; it is a good idea to use a watering can fitted with a fine 'rose' to avoid washing away the seeds.

Annuals which frequently self-seed

Alyssum	Greater quaking grass (*Briza maxima*)	Nasturtium (*Tropaeolum majus*)
Candytuft (*Iberis*)	Marigold (*Calendula*)	Sunflower (*Helianthus*)
Clarkia	Poppy (*Papaver*)	Velvet bent (*Agrostis canina*)
Larkspur (*Consolida*)		

Seedling care

As the seedlings develop their leaves they will benefit from an application of a liquid feed of nitrogen and potash, applied every two weeks, to supplement the phosphates already present in the seedbed. Use a liquid feed rather than a powder or granular formulated fertilizer, to reduce the risk of the seedlings being damaged by excessive nutrient levels.

Many seedlings are easily damaged by early spring frosts, especially in the first few weeks after germination, so as an emergency measure, gently lay sheets of newspaper over the seedlings when frost is forecast – the paper may appear flimsy but its insulation properties can provide seedlings with as much as 2 to 3°C (4 to 5°F) of protection.

Thinning seedlings

After germination the seedlings will probably be too close together and they will need to be thinned out to prevent overcrowding. Remove some seedlings to provide growing room for those which are to remain and mature. Carefully prick out the weakest seedlings or any that are malformed or diseased, leaving well-spaced rows of seedlings.

Transplanting

1 With some plants, particularly vegetables, the seedlings are transplanted and grown in a new plot. Water the bed the night before to moisten the soil. Then using a hand fork, lift the plants out, holding each seedling by its leaves to prevent the stem from getting bruised.

2 In the new plot, make a hole in the soil using a dibber, deep enough to take the roots of the seedling. Place the seedling in the hole and fill in with soil around the base. Finally, gently firm in and water.

Sowing Seeds Indoors

Many summer bedding plants are half-hardy annuals and their seeds would not germinate in garden soil until early summer, as they need extra warmth. Other shrubs, trees and vegetables are perfectly hardy once established, but are frost-tender during their seedling stage and benefit from protection or extra warmth early on. Some seeds also need light to germinate, whereas others must be kept in a dark room with no windows or where the windows have been blacked out.

Seeds which require light

Begonia
Floss flower (*Ageratum*)
Impatiens
Lettuce (*Lactuca sativa*)
Lobelia
Musk (*Mimulus*)
Snapdragon (*Antirrhinum*)
Tobacco plant (*Nicotiana*)

Seeds which require darkness

Amaranthus
Love-in-a-mist (*Nigella*)
Nemesia
Onion (*Allium*)
Pansy (*Viola*)
Phlox
Scorpion weed (*Phacelia*)
Sowbread (*Cyclamen*)

Allium giganteum

Seed sowing

1 Select a seed tray or pot and fill it to the rim with a suitable compost. Firm gently until the compost is 1 cm (½ in) below the rim of the seed tray, and for very fine seeds, such as begonia, sieve an additional thin layer of fine compost over the surface.

2 For fine- and medium-sized seeds, sow broadcast, half in one direction and the remainder in the opposite direction, to ensure even distribution over the tray.

3 For large seeds, create a regular pattern of holes in the compost (you can use a pencil or dibber for this task) and sow the seeds into the prepared holes.

4 Sieve a thin layer of fine compost over the seeds and firm gently. For very fine seeds, simply press them into the surface rather than covering them with more compost.

5 Label and date the seeds. Insert the seed tray into another shallow tray of water and allow the compost to take up water by capillary action; let the surplus water drain away.

Transplanting seedlings

As with seeds sown outdoors, the seedlings will need pricking out and transplanting. This is to remove weak seedlings and to give the remainder more growing space.

1 Select a tray or pot of an appropriate size and fill it to the rim with a suitable compost. Firm gently until the compost is 1 cm (½ in) below the rim of the tray.

2 Using a label or similar utensil, gently tease the seedlings out of the seed compost, making sure you do not damage the roots; hold each seedling up by pinching a leaf between your finger and thumb.

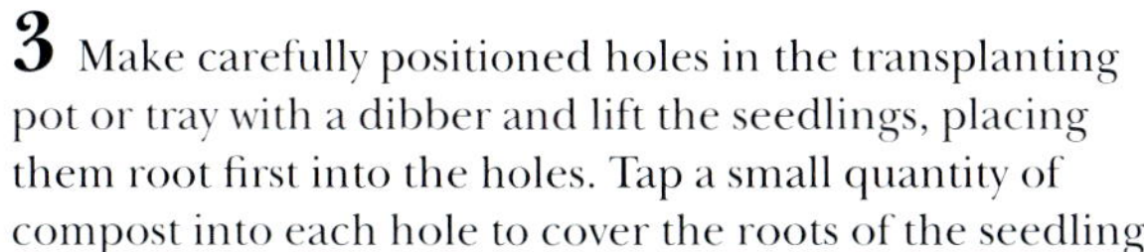

3 Make carefully positioned holes in the transplanting pot or tray with a dibber and lift the seedlings, placing them root first into the holes. Tap a small quantity of compost into each hole to cover the roots of the seedling.

4 When the pot or tray is completed, water each seedling to encourage germination. Use a watering can with a fine 'rose' to settle the compost around the roots without damaging the delicate leaves.

5 Write the name of the plant and the date on a label (this will help you to predict the speed of germination in future years) and insert it in the side of the pot or tray, which should then be placed in a warm, shaded area to aid growth.

Creating a suitable environment

As plants start to grow, they are at their most vulnerable and often need 'intensive care', which means controlling temperature and moisture levels in an enclosed environment.

However, warm humid conditions are an ideal breeding ground for fungal diseases, so make sure you remove any damaged or rotting plants to protect the others.

Protecting seedlings

In many situations a polythene bag or sheet of clingfilm over a plant pot or tray will provide an adequate propagation environment, suitable for many plants, but it is worth remembering that on hot sunny days some form of shading will also be required to prevent sun-scorch.

A more sophisticated alternative is a propagator which is a box-like structure with a base that can be either heated or unheated, and has a transparent cover. Where a heated propagator is used, always try to select one with a thermostatically controlled heater so that you can accurately monitor the temperature.

Cuttings

As the temperature rises and the days lengthen many plants surge into growth and it becomes too late for propagating by hardwood cuttings, as the plants are no longer dormant. For many broad-leaved evergreens and some conifers, it is too early to take semi-ripe cuttings, as the growth is not sufficiently mature. However, many plants can be propagated by softwood cuttings whenever they are in active growth, and for a number of plants the most opportune time is in the spring as the new growth begins.

Softwood cuttings

Select only strong vigorous shoots which are free from obvious signs of pests and disease, and avoid thin or weak shoots that originate from the centre of the plant, as these tend to be too soft and sappy with long internodes (space between the leaf joints).

1 Remove the shoots from the parent plant with a sharp knife or secateurs.

2 If the stem of the cutting is more than 10 cm (4 in) long, reduce it to a length of 7.5–10 cm (3–4 in) by making a cut at right angles to the stem with a sharp knife, cutting 3 mm (⅛ in) below a node.

3 To keep the cuttings fresh and moist, place them in a polythene bag with a few drops of water inside. Keep the bag closed but do not seal it as excess moisture may cause the cutting to wilt.

4 Remove all the leaves from the bottom third of the cutting as they will be of no use and would rot if left attached to the stem.

5 Dip the base of the cuttings into a hormone rooting preparation – this consists of chemicals that are replicas of substances which occur naturally in the plants to promote rooting. Treat *only* the cut surface at the base, as contact with the rooting preparation may cause the soft juvenile bark on the cutting to rot. Tap off any surplus.

6 Select an appropriately sized tray or pot and fill it up with a suitable compost. Remove a little compost from the top so that it sits 2.5 cm (1 in) from the top, but do *not* firm.

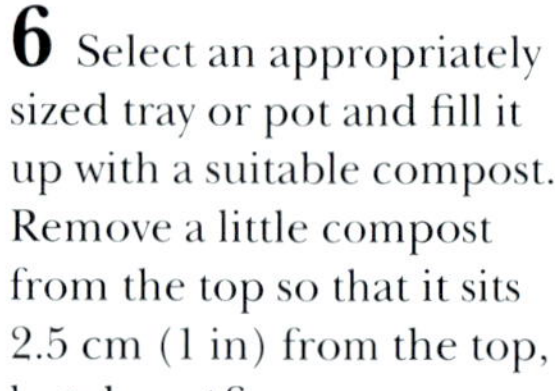

7 Insert the cuttings into the compost by pushing the cuttings, base first, vertically into the free-draining compost, with the bottom third in the compost.

8 When all the cuttings have been inserted, water them gently to settle the compost around the base of the cuttings, without damaging them. The cuttings may appear very loose and floppy for a few days but they will soon recover and look quite healthy, provided they are not allowed to dry out. Write the name of the plant and the date of propagation on a label and insert it at the end of the tray or pot.

9 Place the completed tray or group of pots in a shaded, damp environment to encourage the cuttings to root. With the more difficult subjects, a heated propagator can be used to help promote rapid callus development (healing) and root formation. Place the tray or pots under the cover and control the temperature to create the most suitable environment.

Plants which can be increased by softwood cuttings

Alpines
Alpine pink (*Dianthus alpinus*)
Androsace lanuginosa
Horned violet (*Viola cornuta*)
Hypericum olympicum
Italian bellflower (*Campanula isophylla*)

Shrubs
Abelia schumannii
Caryopteris x *clandonensis*
Ceanothus gloriosus
Forsythia x *intermedia*
Hydrangea paniculata
Mock orange (*Philadelphus coronarius*)

Trees
Caucasian maple (*Acer cappadocicum*)
Erman's birch (*Betula ermanii*)
Eucryphia lucida
Golden-rain tree (*Koelreuteria paniculata*)
Indian bean tree (*Catalpa bignonioides*)
Smooth-leaved elm (*Ulmus minor*)

Perennials
Argyranthemum gracile 'Chelsea girl'
Beardlip penstemon (*Penstemon barbatus*)
Bergamot (*Monarda didyma*)
Clover (*Trifolium*)
Delphinium bellamosum
Mallow (*Lavatera*)
Osteospermum jucundum
Ozark sundrops (*Oenothera macrocarpa*)
Verbena bonariensis

Climbers
Allamanda
Boston ivy (*Parthenocissus tricuspidata*)
Cape ivy (*Senecio macroglossus*)
Clematis montana
Climbing hydrangea (*Hydrangea serrata*)
Japanese wisteria (*Wisteria floribunda*)
Morning glory (*Ipomoea*)
Solanum
Thunbergia
Woodbine (*Lonicera periclymenum*)

Clematis montana

Betula ermanii

Monarda didyma *'Cambridge Scarlet'*

Division

This involves separating large plants into many individual plants or a number of small clumps, which are exact replicas of the parent plant. Many plants are divided when they are dormant but some are better left until the early spring, just before a major growth surge. These include mat- and clump-forming rock plants and suckering shrubs. Snowdrops (*Galanthus*) should also be divided and transplanted soon after flowering, in late spring, rather than in the summer like most bulbs.

Simple division of fibrous-rooted rock plants

Fibrous-rooted plants often form a dense, matted crown which may be difficult to divide without some form of mechanical assistance.

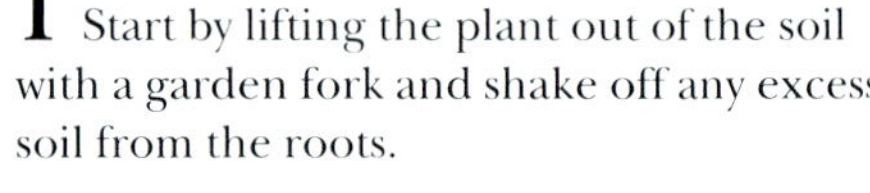

1 Start by lifting the plant out of the soil with a garden fork and shake off any excess soil from the roots.

2 Force the prongs of two garden forks into the centre of the clump so that the forks meet back-to-back at the top of the tines. Apply pressure by pulling the tops of the fork handles together and levering them apart again until the clump starts to tease apart. Repeat this process to create smaller clumps.

3 Any old, woody sections or diseased areas of these clumps should then be cut away and discarded before any replanting takes place. (See page 13 in 'New Introductions' for planting techniques).

Rock plants which can be increased by division

Achillea ageratifolia
Alchemilla mollis
Allium sikkimense
Antennaria dioica
Arenaria montana
Artemesia schmidtiana 'Nana'
Chiastophyllum oppositifolium
Fairies' thimbles (*Campanula cochlearifolia*)
Garden violet (*Viola odorata*)
Gentiana sino-ornata
Golden creeping Jenny (*Lysimachia nummularia*)
Oxalis adenophylla
Primula (*Primula*)
Pulsatilla
Saxifraga apiculata
Sedum kamtschaticum

Gentiana sino-ornata

Alchemilla mollis

Pulsatilla

Simple division of suckering shrubs

1 Dig carefully around the shrub with a fork and ease a section of root, with suckers on it, out of the ground.

2 Cut this section from the main plant with secateurs or a sharp knife, making sure it has plenty of fibrous roots on it.

3 To prepare the root for planting, remove the leaves from the top section of the cutting.

4 Dig a planting hole for the shrub's root system, breaking up the soil in the base of the hole to encourage deep root penetration from the new plant.

5 Replant the sucker, firm in around the base and water thoroughly.

Suckering shrubs which can be increased by division

Amelanchier lamarkii
Berberis buxifolia
Bush honeysuckle (*Diervilla lonicera*)
Butcher's broom (*Ruscus aculeatus*)
Cassiope lycopodioides
Creeping dogwood (*Cornus canadensis*)
Euonymus fortunei
Gaultheria mucronata
Glory flower (*Clerodendrum bungei*)
Kerria japonica
Mahonia repens
Polygala chamaebuxus
Red chokeberry (*Aronia arbutifolia*)
Sarcococca humilis
Spiraea japonica
Sweetspire (*Itea virginica*)

Division of snowdrops

1 After the flowers have died off, lift clumps up with a hand fork, making sure you do not damage the bulbs with the tines of the fork.

2 Shake the soil from the roots so you can see what you are doing and then carefully divide the clump, pulling out individual bulbs. Make sure there are roots and leaves attached to each bulb.

3 Pull any bulblets away from the parent bulb – these can be replanted as well if they are in a good condition and will simply take longer to develop than the main sections of bulb.

4 Replant the bulbs in the same depth of soil as they were originally planted. (See page 11 for planting techniques.)

Layering

This is ideal for plants which are difficult to root or would need specialist knowledge and facilities to make rooting cuttings a realistic proposition. Very simply, the method involves the formation of new shoots on the new plant, before it is separated from the parent plant.

The principles of layering

A whole range of plants can be propagated by layering, provided the correct method is used, as some plants have slightly different requirements. There are three basic treatments: the first includes simple, serpentine and tip layering and involves planting a section of the stem into the soil; the second is stooling which involves mounding soil over the stem; the third method, used for stiff or high branches, is referred to as air layering.

Simple layering

1 In spring, select a strong, healthy shoot of the previous season's growth and bend it down into a horizontal position. Two-thirds of the way along the shoot make a mark in the soil.

2 Where the soil has been marked, dig an oval-shaped hole about 15 cm (6 in) deep, using a trowel.

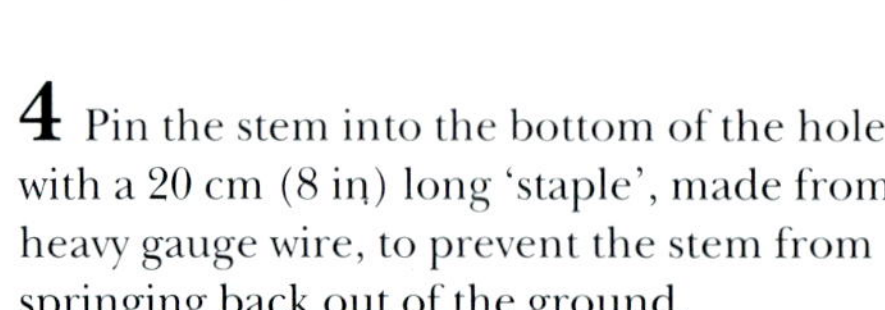

3 With a sharp knife, scrape away a 2.5 cm (1 in) long section of bark to cause a wound on the section of stem to be buried. Bring down the shoot into a horizontal position and gently bend it into the prepared hole.

4 Pin the stem into the bottom of the hole with a 20 cm (8 in) long 'staple', made from heavy gauge wire, to prevent the stem from springing back out of the ground.

5 Fill the hole with soil and firm gently. Water the soil if it becomes dry, to keep the stem moist and encourage roots to form.

6 In late winter, remove the soil and expose the roots which have formed at the base of each shoot. Cut off these new plants with as much root as possible and a small section of stem; they can now be replanted. (See 'New Introductions', on pages 8–25 for planting.)

Serpentine layering

This is a variation on simple layering, used for vigorous plants with long flexible stems, such as clematis, climbing roses and lonicera. This technique has the advantage that one stem can yield as many as five or six plants, rather than just the single plant per stem which is obtained by simple layering.

Follow the method used for 'Simple layering', but make several wounds on one long trailing shoot, in between buds, and peg down each wounded section leaving the section of stem in between exposed. Once they have rooted, cut each rooted section into an individual plant, ready for replanting.

Tip layering

Some plants naturally layer themselves; they have long arching stems which curve down to the ground, and where the tip of the stem comes into contact with the soil, adventitious roots form and grow into the soil. This can be encouraged by using a trowel to bury these tips about 15 cm (6 in) deep into the soil, so that a better root system is formed. In the late autumn, sever the rooted layer from the parent plant, lift the new plants and transplant them.

Stooling

Stooling, or mound layering, is often used to produce large numbers of plants, or rejuvenate an old plant which has become tall and straggly or bare and open in the centre.

1 In the early spring, cut down the plant to a height of about 5 cm (2 in) and remove and discard all of the top growth.

2 The plant responds to this treatment by producing lots of new shoots. When these reach 10–15 cm (4–6 in) high, rake up soil to form a mound about 5–7.5 cm (2–3 in) high around the base of each shoot.

3 Repeat this process in the summer when the shoots are 30 cm (12 in) high, and again when they are 45 cm (18 in) high; each time the bottom half of the shoots are covered until the mound is about 20 cm (8 in) high.

4 In late autumn or early winter, carefully remove the mound of soil and expose the roots which will now have formed at the base of each shoot.

5 Once all of the soil has been removed, cut off these new plants with as much root as possible, but always leave a short stub of growth on the parent plant, as this is where the next layers will emerge. These plants can now be potted or planted out in the garden.

Air layering

This method of propagation is used for plants with high branches or stiff shoots, which cannot be lowered to soil level without breaking.

1 Choose a section of branch consisting of the current season's growth and clear any leaves or side shoots along a 15 cm (6 in) stretch, starting about 30 cm (12 in) down from the shoot tip.

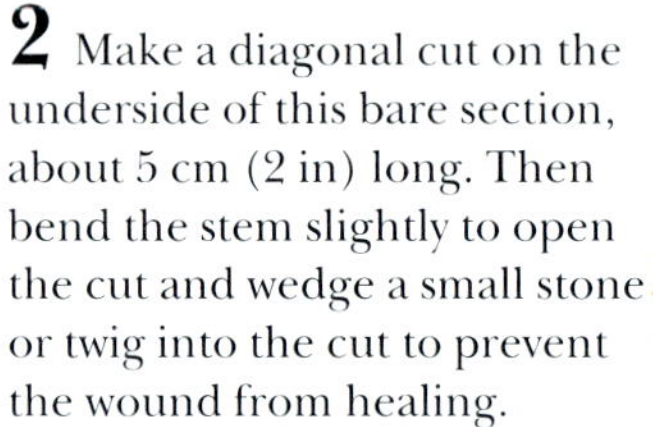

2 Make a diagonal cut on the underside of this bare section, about 5 cm (2 in) long. Then bend the stem slightly to open the cut and wedge a small stone or twig into the cut to prevent the wound from healing.

3 Cut the bottom out of a polythene bag, pull it over the stem and tie the bottom end about 5 cm (2 in) below the cut.

4 Fill the polythene sleeve with moist, open compost, making sure that there is plenty of compost around the cut. Fasten the top of the sleeve about 10 cm (4 in) above the cut and then leave the sleeve on the plant for about 12 weeks to allow roots to form in the cut.

5 Finally, untie and carefully remove the polythene sleeve, without damaging any of the delicate new roots. Cut off the shoot just below the newly formed root ball and plant it in a pot of compost (see New Introductions on pages 8–25 for planting techniques). It is essential you keep the freshly rooted plant well watered until it is fully established or the roots will die.

Plants suitable for simple, serpentine and tip layering

Blackberry (*Rubus*)
Clematis
Corylopsis
Hazel (*Corylus*)
Honeysuckle (*Lonicera*)
Hops (*Humulus*)
Ivy (*Hedera*)
Winter jasmine (*Jasminum nudiflorum*)
Wisteria

Plants suitable for stooling

Apple (*Malus*)
Flowering currant (*Ribes*)
Heath (*Erica*)
Lavender (*Lavandula angustifolia*)
Smoke bush (*Cotinus*)
Willow (*Salix*)
Wormwood (*Artemisia absinthium*)

Plants suitable for air layering

Bay laurel (*Laurus nobilis*)
Calico bush (*Kalmia latifolia*)
Chinese witch hazel (*Hamamelis mollis*)
Common holly (*Ilex aquifolium*)
Dove tree (*Davidia involucrata*)

Grafting

This method of propagation involves a process of joining separate plants together; the upper part or 'scion' is a section of stem taken from the plant which is to be increased in numbers, and the lower part or 'rootstock' needs to be as closely related to the scion as possible. Grafting is ideal for plants which are slow to root or will not produce roots of their own.

Whip and tongue grafting

It is possible to propagate most plants successfully with whip and tongue grafting, which is the most frequently used and simplest method of permanently interlocking two plants. All you need to begin is a good quality, sharp knife and a little practice.

1 To get the scion, select a healthy shoot of the current season's growth and remove it from the parent plant using a pair of secateurs.

Trim the scion into a 10–15 cm (4–6 in) length; the top cut is made just above a bud and the bottom cut is made just below one.

2 Having chosen your rootstock, prepare it by making a flat cut across its top, 15–20 cm (6–8 in) above soil level.

3 On the upper section of the rootstock, make a shallow upward slanting cut approximately 7.5 cm (3 in) long on one side.

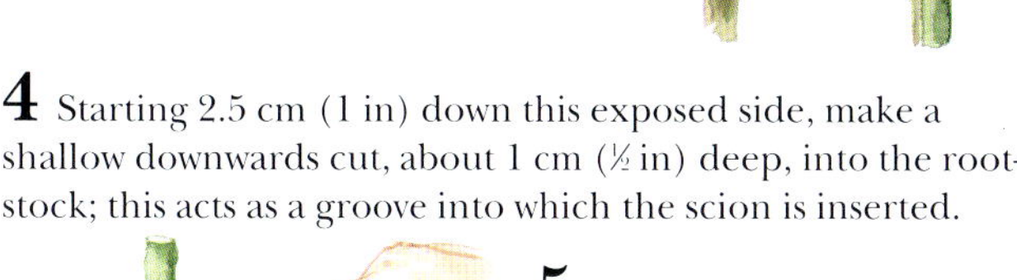

4 Starting 2.5 cm (1 in) down this exposed side, make a shallow downwards cut, about 1 cm (½ in) deep, into the rootstock; this acts as a groove into which the scion is inserted.

5 Now prepare the scion in the same way by making a slanting cut approximately 7.5 cm (3 in) long on the bottom section.

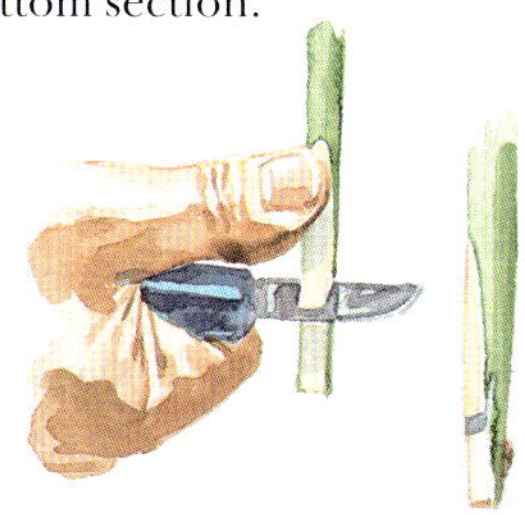

6 Then 2.5 cm (1 in) from the bottom of this cut surface, make another cut upwards, 1 cm (½ in) deep, (try to avoid handling the cut surface) to match the groove in the rootstock.

7 Place the scion and rootstock together so that the cut surfaces match and the grooves interlock.

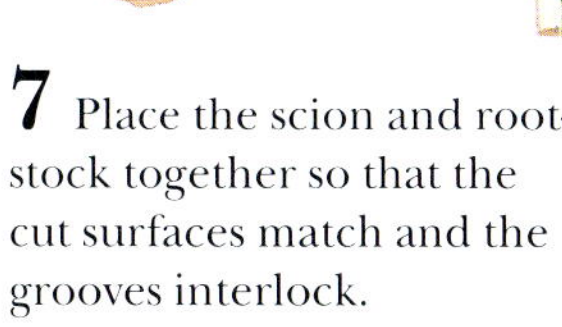

8 Bind the graft with waterproof plastic tape. After 3 or 4 weeks when the stems start to heal together, slit the tape and allow it to split open.

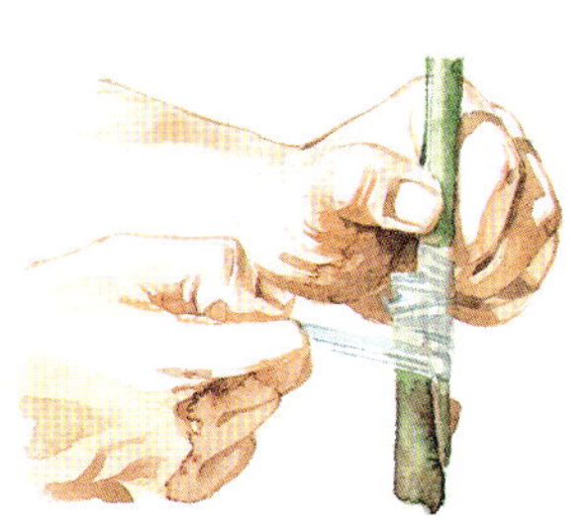

seasonal pruning

In the early stages of a plant's life the main reason for pruning is to create a structural framework of branches. Many plants also need pruning to sustain or improve the quality of their fruit, flowers, leaves or stems. A special pruning technique, known as 'renovation' pruning', is used to rejuvenate a plant which has become neglected, overgrown or old, restoring it to good health and a more manageable size. In many respects, spring pruning is an ideal time to take a close look at the plants in your garden and assess how good their condition actually is. This close scrutiny will also provide the opportunity to examine the plants for frost damage, especially after a cold period with frozen ground and drying winds.

Getting Started

The key to good pruning is to work with the plant, using the natural growth pattern of the plant you are pruning to get the best results. Always stand back and assess the whole plant before making any cuts, have an overall plan of what you hope to achieve, and try to have in your mind an image of how the plant should look when the pruning has been completed, paying particular attention to size and shape.

Pruning tools

Select the right pruning tools by looking at the size of the branch or stem to be cut – using tools that are too small can result in poor ragged cuts, damage to the tools and injury to the gardener. Tools that are too large will make the job more difficult.

Secateurs

For shoots and stems of 1 cm (½ in) to 2.5 cm (1 in) in diameter, secateurs are the tool most commonly used, as they cut through both soft green tissue and tougher woody material. There are several types available: anvil secateurs have a single straight-edged cutting blade that closes down onto an anvil – a bar of softer metal; a ratchet type that cuts the branch in stages is very good for reducing fatigue; and the parrot-bill type has two curved blades that bypass one another very closely and cut in a scissor-like action.

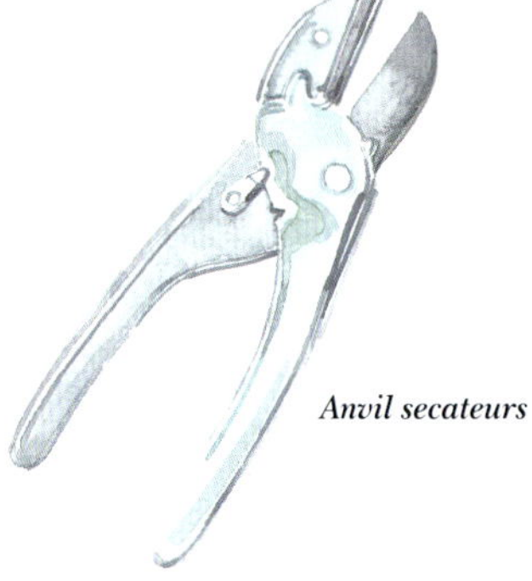

Anvil secateurs

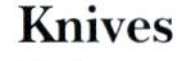

Shears

Shears are available in several designs, but they should be strong, light and comfortable to use, with a sharp cutting edge. Most have straight blades with a deep notch at the base for cutting thicker stems.

Knives

Knives can be used for light trimming and dead-heading of flowers. A general-purpose knife with a straight blade is good enough for most jobs, but special pruning knives with curved blades are designed for better control.

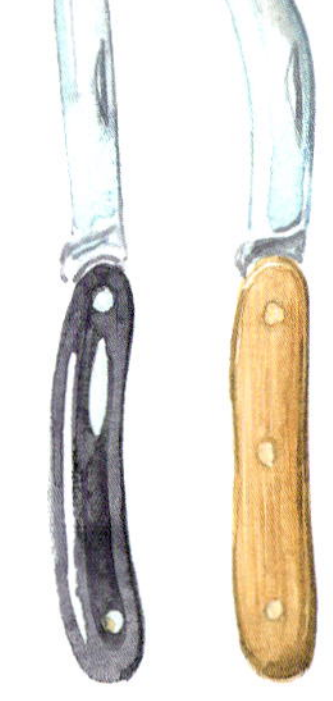

Ordinary and curved blades.

Maintain the shape of Clematis viticella *'Madame Julia Correvon' with secateurs.*

Taxus baccata *may need trimming with shears to keep a neat overall appearance.*

Use shears to control any wayward growth on Hedera helix *'Goldheart'.*

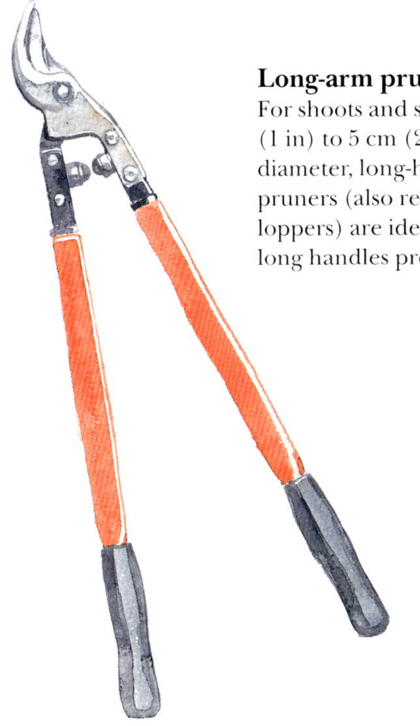

Long-arm pruners
For shoots and stems 2.5 cm (1 in) to 5 cm (2 in) in diameter, long-handled pruners (also referred to as loppers) are ideal, as the long handles provide extra leverage which makes cutting through thicker stems easier and also avoids any damage to secateurs or injury to the gardener's fingers and wrists.

Long-handled pruners
Use for tree branches which would normally be out of reach; these will cut through branches up to 3 cm (1¼ in) thick. They consist of a pole 2–3 m (6½–10 ft) in length, with a hooked anvil and curved blade at the tip, with the blade being operated by a lever at the opposite end.

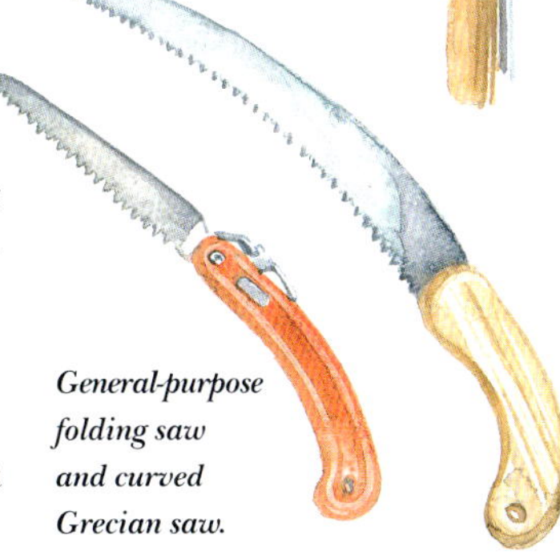

Pruning saws
For shoots and stems of more than 5 cm (2 in) in diameter, or dead wood (often difficult to cut with secateurs and loppers), a pruning saw is the best tool to use. Many of these saws are designed to fold up and fit neatly into a pocket when not in use. General-purpose pruning saws have a tapering blade with teeth on one side, to cut on both the push and return stroke. The Grecian saw has a curved blade tapered to a sharp point and sloping teeth designed to cut on the return stroke.

General-purpose folding saw and curved Grecian saw.

Principles of pruning and training

Pruning produces vegetative or shoot growth, which is why we prune in the first place. The apical bud (growing point) of a stem is usually dominant over the growth buds immediately below it – pruning to remove the tips of dominant growth buds, therefore, results in the development of more vigorous growth buds or flowering shoots further down the stem. 'Prune weak growth hard but prune strong growth lightly' is an adage to bear in mind when correcting the appearance of a misshapen plant.

Reach the uppermost branches of Ilex x altaclarensis *using special long-arm pruners.*

Catalpa bignonioides *'Aurea' is a good subject for pollarding, which can be done with a saw.*

Long-handled pruners will enable you to reach the top of a Prunus laurocerasus.

Roses

The rose is one of the most popular garden plants in the world, due mainly to the wide range of growth habits, scents and flower colours which are available. Being quite easy to grow, they are a group of plants that are very popular with both beginners and experienced gardeners alike. The purpose of pruning roses is to cut out the older, less vigorous stems which will help to encourage the development of strong vigorous new growth that is disease-free and will produce better quality flowers.

Pruning cuts

Cut 5 mm (¼ in) above a bud.

Pruning cuts must be clean, with no crushing of the tissue or ragged edges, at an angle slanting slightly away from the bud to reduce the risk of secondary damage from disease infection. Use sharp secateurs, or, for particularly thick stems a pruning saw or long-handled loppers.

Cut to an outward-pointing bud to encourage an open-centred habit in bush roses, or with roses of spreading habit, prune some branches to inward-pointing buds for more upright growth. Make sure you cut back until you reach healthy, white wood – anything discoloured or brown is likely to be dead.

Outward-pointing buds.

Spring pruning

Not all roses require a spring pruning, but for those that do (see opposite), this is best carried out just before the plants come out of dormancy – earlier pruning can cause too much early growth, which is often damaged by the weather, and later pruning often involves wasting the plant's energy by cutting off young growth that has already been produced. If you are unsure when to prune, the best advice is to prune when the growth buds halfway up the most vigorous stems are just beginning to swell.

Rosa *'Deep Secret'*

Rosa *'Iceberg'*

Rosa *'Empress Josephine'*

Frost damage

This can occur with fluctuating spring weather, where warm spells are followed by frosty periods. If the new shoots are damaged by frost, cut them back to healthy dormant buds further back on the main stems, making sure you remove all the dead wood. If there is a chance that frosts may return, particularly at the beginning of spring, then leave the damaged stem in place until the danger has passed.

Modern bush roses

Modern bush roses, particularly those grown in colder climates, will have been pruned in the autumn to reduce wind-rock. Once the danger of frost has passed in the following spring, they can be pruned normally. Most modern roses flower on the current season's wood, which means many of them need to be pruned quite severely in spring or they tend to become very tall and 'leggy' with the flowers forming high on the plant.

Miniature roses

Slow-growing miniature roses will flower for many years with little or no formal pruning; simply cut out dead, diseased or damaged stems. The only planned pruning required is to prevent them from spreading too far by cutting long shoots well back into their allotted area to an upward-facing bud.

Miniature roses	
Rosa 'Arizona Sunset'	*Rosa* 'Peaches n' Cream'
Rosa 'Darling Flame'	*Rosa* 'Snowball'
	Rosa 'Yellow Doll'

Hybrid tea and floribunda roses

Hybrid tea (large-flowered bush roses) and floribundas (cluster-flowered bush roses) are pruned in a similar way. Remove any thick stumps or unproductive growth to ground level. The remaining stems are cut back to 15 cm (6 in) for hybrid tea roses, and to 20–25 cm (8–10 in) for floribunda roses.

Hybrid tea	Floribunda
Rosa 'Alexander'	*Rosa* 'Arthur Bell'
Rosa 'Deep Secret'	*Rosa* 'Iceberg'
Rosa 'Freedom'	*Rosa* 'The Queen Elizabeth'
Rosa 'Royal William'	

Shrub, species and old garden roses

Just about all of the species and most of the shrub roses, both old and modern, flower on wood which is two years or more in age, and many will flower very well for a number of years without any pruning. The removal of weak, dead, damaged and diseased wood, followed by a light pruning, is normally required in the autumn however.

The exceptions to this are modern shrub roses, such as *Rosa rugosa* and its respective hybrids, which should be pruned in early spring. The densely formed Gallica roses also benefit from a spring pruning. Remove all dead, diseased and damaged growth and tip prune any over-vigorous shoots.

Modern shrub roses	Gallica roses
Rosa rugosa 'Agnes'	*Rosa* 'Belle de Crecy'
Rosa rugosa 'Fimbriata'	*Rosa* 'Duc de Guiche'
	Rosa 'Tuscany Superb'

Climbing and Wall Plants

True climbers are plants that can support themselves in a vertical position, with the natural support usually being some form of plant modification which has evolved to grasp or cling onto other plants or structures. These clinging devices may take the form of twining stems, tendrils, thorns and sucker pads or roots. When considering the pruning and training of wall shrubs and climbers, it is important to observe the growth and flowering habit of your plants.

Formative pruning

This will need to be done on all newly planted climbers to maintain a balanced framework for maximum coverage.

With a vigorous climber, such as wisteria, the key to success is to ensure that new vigorous shoots are produced in the spring.

1 Remove any growth damaged by frost or wind, and prune back the tip of each shoot to a strong healthy bud. Often these shoots are cut back to 30 cm (12 in) to encourage new growths to develop from close to the base of the plant. Train in the young growths as they develop and prune back the tips of any excessively vigorous shoots.

2 Climbers with aerial roots or sucker pads, such as ivy (*Hedera*) and Virginia creeper (*Parthenocissus*) are capable of supporting themselves, but they will almost certainly need some initial help and encouragement to grow close to the support until they are able to attach themselves to the wall or fence. This also applies to wall shrubs. Use guiding canes, fanned out against a wall or reaching up to a section of trellis, and tie in the new shoots with garden twine.

Clematis *'Ernest Markham'*

Hedera helix *'Cristata'*

Clematis *'Comtesse de Bouchaud'*

Routine pruning

To maintain the health and vigour of your climber, as well as keep its shape, a certain amount of maintenance pruning is necessary. The first pruning is carried out in the summer, after flowering, and the second when the plant is dormant, to reduce over-long laterals. There are exceptions however; evergreens, unless they flower on the previous season's growth, prefer a spring pruning, as do certain types of clematis.

Evergreens

Those that flower on the current season's growth should be pruned in early spring. Remove all weak growth, damaged and badly congested stems and re-tie the shoots.

Spring pruning evergreen climbers

Birthwort (*Aristolochia*)
Cissus
Distictis
Ivy (*Hedera*)
Passion flower (*Passiflora*)
Trachelospermum

Group 2 clematis

Flowers are produced on stems of up to 60 cm (2 ft) which develop from the previous season's stems. Remove any dead, damaged or weak growth and cut back healthy stems to just above a strong pair of leaf buds which will produce the flowering shoots. Clematis in this group may produce a second flush of blooms in late summer. This habit can be exploited by pruning half of the shoots much harder in the spring, to encourage a more prominent later flush of flowers and so extend the flowering season.

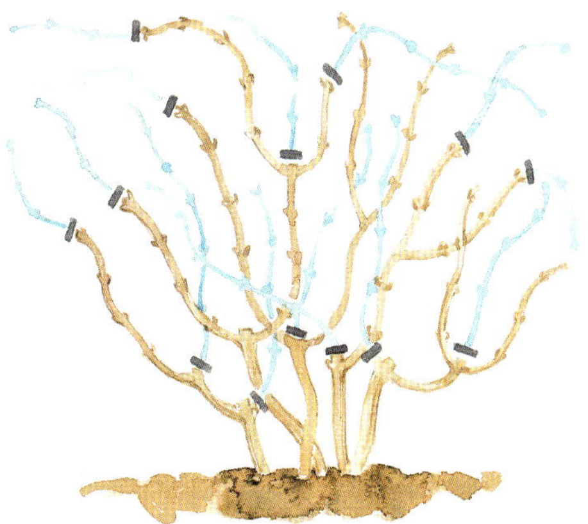

Clematis that flower from early June to early July

Clematis 'Barbara Jackman'	*Clematis* 'Lasurstern'
Clematis 'Carnaby'	*Clematis* 'Marie Boisselot'
Clematis 'Daniel Deronda'	*Clematis* 'Mrs N. Thompson'
Clematis 'Duchess of Edinburgh'	*Clematis* 'Nelly Moser'
Clematis 'Elsa Spath'	*Clematis* 'Vyvyan Pennell'
Clematis 'Henryi'	

Group 3 clematis

The plants in this group produce flowers on stems of the current season's growth, and respond best when pruned in early spring before growth starts. The method simply involves cutting down all of the stems to a pair of buds, within 45 cm (18 in) of ground level, usually just above the start of the previous season's growth. Once the plant has been cut down, the stems will start to form new brittle growth which will need to be trained in until the tendrils can take over.

Clematis that flower from early July to October

Clematis 'Duchess of Albany'	*Clematis* 'Hagley Hybrid'
Clematis florida	*Clematis* 'Lady Betty Balfour'
Clematis 'Gipsy Queen'	*Clematis tangutica*
Clematis 'Jackmanii'	*Clematis viticella*

Shrubs

There are a small number of shrubs which will hardly ever need pruning; they are usually the broad-leaved evergreens, such as *Cotoneaster conspicuus*, *Ruscus aculeatus* and *Sarcococca humilis*. However, by far the greater number of shrubs, if left to grow naturally, will eventually become overgrown and look unattractive, and will deteriorate over a period of time as the overall growth suffers and the health of the shrub declines.

Pruning cuts

Any pruning cut you make should be at an angle, 5 mm (¼ in) above a bud, with the bud itself positioned near the high point of the cut. This is very important because rapid healing is greatly accelerated by the close proximity of the growth buds.

Formative pruning

Deciduous shrubs usually require more formative pruning than evergreen ones which tend to grow naturally in an upright and even way. Carry out pruning when the plant is dormant, between late autumn and mid-spring, or soon after planting. Cut back the stems to outward-facing buds to form a strong framework.

Routine pruning

Deciduous shrubs
Those that flower early in the year on the previous season's wood, such as *Prunus triloba*, *Leycesteria*, *Abutilon* and Russian sage (*Perovskia*), are best pruned hard in spring, to within 5 cm (2 in) of ground level, giving the flowering wood time to develop.

Less vigorous shrubs that flower on the current season's growth, such as *Cotinus*, *Fuchsia*, *Hibiscus* and mallow (*Lavatera*), should be cut back in spring to within 30 cm (12 in) of ground level, to keep the basic framework intact. Also remove weak and damaged stems.

Evergreen shrubs

For winter- or spring-flowering shrubs, such as *Berberis darwinii* and *Viburnum tinus*, prune immediately after flowering. Others, such as *Olearia macrodonta* and *Osmanthus heterophyllus*, which flower from midsummer onwards, are pruned in mid-spring.

Remove all dead, diseased or damaged wood and any thin straggly shoots. Cut back flower stems to a healthy bud and reduce the length of any strong vigorous shoots affecting the shape and balance of the plant.

Remedial pruning

Old, neglected or badly shaped shrubs often respond to severe pruning, which can be used to renovate plants as they produce young growth from the base. Early spring is the best time to carry out this treatment on evergreens – deciduous shrubs are best renovated during the dormant season (autumn and winter). Not all shrubs will take kindly to this treatment, for instance, broom (*Cytisus*) will die rather than produce new growths when pruned in this way. For these types of plants cut out only a proportion of the main stems, and remove the remaining old growths after flowering in summer or the following winter. For a badly diseased plant, however, replacement may be the only option.

First year

Cut back the main stems to within 30 cm (1 ft) of the ground in order to promote new growth from the base of the plant.

Second year

Cut back the new shoots to their point of origin, leaving only 2 or 3 of the strongest and best placed shoots to create a balanced framework.

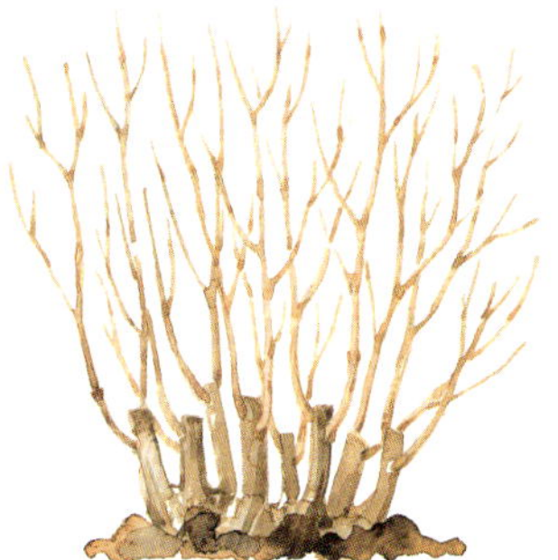

Subsequent years

In the third and subsequent years, prune according to the technique appropriate to your shrub as part of a normal growing cycle.

Magnolia

Lavandula angustifolia

Camellia reticulata

Evergreens that respond well to renovation pruning

Berberis darwinii
Box (*Buxus sempervirens*)
Camellia
Cherry laurel (*Prunus laurocerasus*)
Cistus x *corbariensis*
Cotoneaster congestus
Ilex x *altaclerensis*
Lavandula angustifolia
Magnolia grandiflora
Spotted laurel (*Aucuba japonica*)

Trees

Routine pruning is normally carried out in the dormant season, when trees often naturally prune themselves as weak growths break off. Also, some trees will bleed heavily if pruned in spring, such as Norway maple (*Acer platanoides*), silver birch (*Betula pendula*) and black walnut (*Juglans nigra*). Others, however, benefit from crown reduction and thinning in the spring to correct their shape and improve their health, and coppicing and pollarding now can create a colourful winter display on trees such as willow (*Salix*).

Crown reduction

Often referred to as crown shaping, this involves an overall reduction of the crown to even out the profile by shortening the branches back to growing points, which will encourage regrowth to occur. Pruning on the stronger sections of the crown will consist mainly of tipping shoots by pruning back the end third of each shoot – more severe pruning is counter productive as it will encourage vigorous growth. On the weaker sections of the crown, pruning can be more severe, with some branches being cut back by about two-thirds of their length to encourage strong vigorous growth.

Crown thinning

Crown thinning initially involves the removal of thin, weak and crossing branches, followed by the complete or partial removal of selected healthy branches to achieve an overall reduction in the density of the canopy. Ideally, crown thinning should be carried out on the branch tips with very few large branches being removed, unless it is absolutely essential. This operation will have the effect of reducing the density of the foliage but not changing the overall profile of the canopy. One advantage of this technique is that more light reaches the centre of the tree, often leading to dormant buds on the main branches producing new shoots.

Arbutus unedo

Trees that benefit from crown reduction and thinning

- Hognut (*Carya glabra*)
- Indian bean tree (*Catalpa bignonioides*)
- Katsura tree (*Cercidophyllum japonicum*)
- Pencil cedar (*Juniperus virginiana*)
- Red oak (*Quercus rubra*)
- Strawberry tree (*Arbutus unedo*)

Coppicing

This technique of hard pruning is a traditional method of managing specimens such as sweet chestnut (*Castanea sativa*), to give a constant and renewable supply of shoots. Using pruning loppers, the plants are cut back in the spring to about 5–8 cm (2–3 in) above ground level; new shoots will develop from this woody base.

Salix alba *'Britzensis'*

Trees suitable for coppicing

Acer cappadocicum 'Aureum'
Common hornbeam (*Carpinus betulus*)
Corylus avellana 'Purpurea'
Mountain gum (*Eucalyptus dalrympleana*)
Salix alba 'Britzensis'
Yew (*Taxus baccata*)

Pollarding

This severe pruning technique produces lots of thin, whippy new growths with young branches that have an attractive bark in the winter. A small canopy of branches will be created that do not cast dense shadows on the ground.

1 To develop a pollarded tree, the plant is allowed to grow as a single stem until it reaches a desired height of about 1.8 m (6 ft). In the early spring, all of the side branches are removed to leave stubs of growth 5 cm (2 in) long.

2 This severe pruning will lead to a mass of new shoots developing in the spring and summer, and some of these branches may need thinning to prevent weak stems forming, due to overcrowding. Cut these off making sure the remaining stems are strong and healthy as well as being evenly spaced to create a well balanced display. Any shoots which form on the trunk will need to be cut off as they emerge, as these will spoil the effect of the pollard.

3 Pollarding is essentially an ornamental type of pruning, but it is also a useful technique to use on older trees that have become over grown or are in need of some form of rejuvenation. It is usually carried out every other year as this will help to keep the tree in good condition but will have the effect of draining away too much of its natural vigour – this is especially important during the first 5 years of establishment in newly planted trees.

Acer pensylvanicum

Trees suitable for pollarding

Acer cappadocicum 'Aureum'
Acer pensylvanicum
Judas tree (*Cercis siliquastrum*)
Populus alba 'Richardii'
Populus x *candicans* 'Aurora'
Salix alba 'Britzensis'
Salix daphnoides 'Aglaia'
Salix matsudana 'Tortuosa'
Salix x *sepulcralis* 'Erythroflexuosa'
Taxus baccata
White mulberry (*Morus alba*)

lawn care

The condition of the spring lawn will depend almost entirely on how severe the preceding winter has been, and how well the grass has survived the cold weather. In the spring, as the days get longer and the temperature gradually begins to rise, the grass will slowly start to grow and mowing the lawn will become a regular task. To sustain this rapid growth, the lawn will need to be fed and the weeds checked or killed. At the beginning of the season there is usually the need to carry out some repair work, with hollows forming as the soil lifts and settles due to frost heave, and edges that have crumbled away or been trodden down. This is also a good time to introduce plants into your lawn to add a new level of interest.

The Essentials

There are a number of tools you will need to keep your lawn in optimum condition. The size and type of lawn you have will dictate some of your choices. However, the one maintenance tool everyone needs is a mower, as regular mowing to the correct height prevents the grass from becoming yellow and uneven and also prevents scalping.

Cutting equipment

For mowing the lawn the cylinder and rotary types are both capable of creating a striped effect if fitted with a roller behind the cutting blades; and the hover is useful for creating an even cut on awkward-shaped lawns. Other manual tools are used for neatening the edges, either by cutting through the turf or clipping the grass.

Cylinder mowers
Cylinder mowers have a number of spirally arranged cutting blades that form a cylinder. These rotating blades cut against a fixed blade in a scissor-like action. They are manual or powered.

Rotary mowers
These have one or more blades, or a toughened nylon cord which rotates horizontally at very high speed, slicing through the grass. They work particularly well on long or tough grass.

Hover mowers
Hover mowers are similar to rotary type mowers except that they ride on a cushion of air. They are light and easy to use and particularly good for small lawns and awkward shaped lawns.

Edging shears
These are shears which have handles set at right angles to the cutting blades, and are used for trimming the grass growing over the lawn edge from a standing position.

Half-moon edger
This special tool is used for cutting turf and trimming lawn edges. The curved blade is mounted onto a spade shaft and handle, making it easy to use.

General equipment

A garden fork is ideal for easing, lifting and spiking the lawn, using the tines to alleviate soil compaction. To rake out moss, collect leaves and remove debris from the lawn, use a fan rake, and for scattering dew, spreading top dressing and breaking up worm casts, use a stiff brush. A fertilizer spreader is another useful piece of equipment for applying powdered fertilizer evenly.

Watering equipment

Static sprinkler
A spinning head distributes water in a circular pattern; the area covered depends on the water pressure.

Rotary sprinkler
The rotating arms provide an even distribution over a wide area (depending on water pressure). Some have adjustable nozzles to regulate the size of the water droplets.

Oscillating sprinkler
A tube with nozzles mounted in a line provides a fan-shaped water pattern. The arm is driven from side-to-side in an arc, spraying water. The speed of rotation is governed by water pressure.

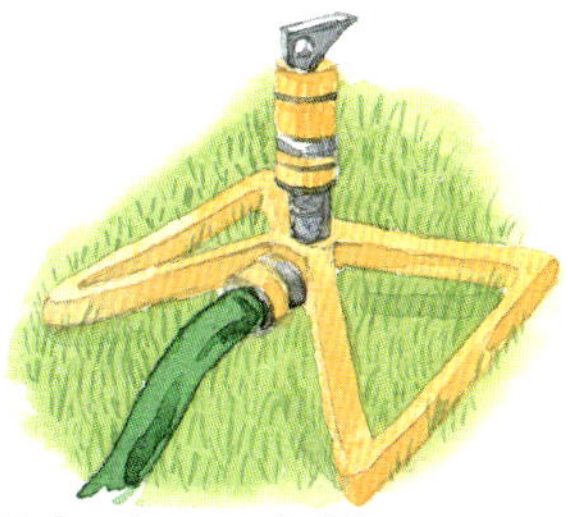

Pulse-jet sprinkler
A nozzle rotates in a series of pulses, distributing an arc of water to cover all, or parts of a circular pattern.

Lay-flat sprinkler hose
A flattened hosepipe punctured with a series of holes provides a fine spray over the grass at high pressure, or at low pressure the water weeps gently from the hose. This system is useful for watering in areas with low water pressure.

Post winter cutting

1 As soon as the grass shows signs of new growth, use a fan rake to rake away all traces of dead grass, debris and worm casts which have accumulated on the lawn during the winter.

2 The grass may be quite long at the beginning of spring so trying to cut the lawn too low may result in clogging the mower, damaging the machine and scalping the grass, the latter of which may encourage moss and weeds to grow in the lawn. To avoid this, set the blades on the highest possible setting to encourage growth from the base and root development.

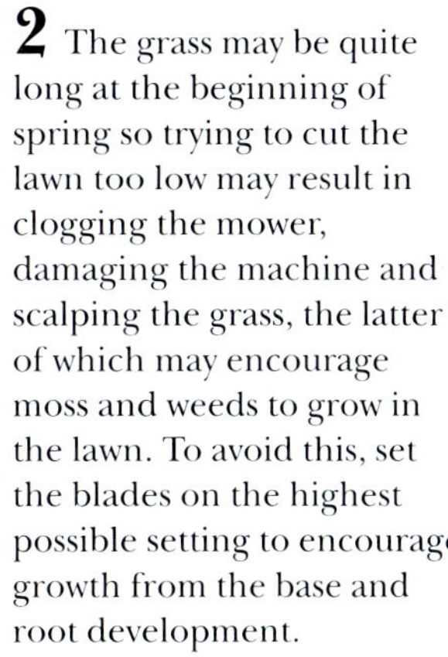

3 Choose a dry day to mow your lawn as wet grass can produce an untidy effect once it has dried out. Check that there are no stones or branches on the lawn and start mowing by moving forward at a steady pace.

4 Take away the grass clippings. Clean and store the mower, and lower the mower blades ready for the next cut, which will need to be done in about a week.

5 The lawn edge is then re-cut at the beginning of the season with a half-moon edger to redefine the perimeter of the lawn. Place a plank on the edge of the lawn as a guide and to protect the grass. After this, keep the edge trimmed with edging shears.

General Maintenance

There are several important tasks you can carry out to maintain a high quality lawn. The surface may need aerating to improve oxygen levels around the roots and help growth, which can be further helped with the addition of lawn fertilizer. As the season progresses, warmth and humidity increase and this encourages the spread of weeds, which must be eradicated immediately.

Feeding

As mowing becomes more frequent, the continual removal of vegetation from the lawn means that important plant nutrients are lost when the grass clippings are taken away. This loss of food will need to be replaced with lawn fertilizer.

Preparing the lawn

A spring dressing should be applied as soon as the grass shows visible signs of growth. A dry or compacted lawn should be well watered before the fertilizer is applied, as this ensures that it penetrates the soil and reaches the roots quickly.

Methods of application

If applying by hand, on a dry day, mark the lawn into plots and measure the fertilizer into the correct amount for each plot. Then scatter the fertilizer evenly over each area.

If using an applicator, check the setting and load the fertilizer into the hopper. Walk steadily across the lawn for an even application, at the rate recommended by the manufacturer. Clean out the applicator thoroughly after use.

Irrigate if there is no rain during the first 2 days after application, as the grass roots can become damaged if there are high concentrations of dry fertilizer left around them for long periods.

Types of fertilizer

Spring fertilizers contain high levels of nitrogen which are needed to promote strong, vigorous growth. Clay soils will need less fertilizer than light sandy ones, which tend to lose nutrients through leaching.

The mixture in the table opposite contains both slow- and fast-acting fertilizers for a constant supply of organic and inorganic nutrients – many proprietary fertilizers will contain some or all of these materials.

A typical spring lawn feed

Fertilizer	**kg per 100 sq metres (lb per 120 sq yards)**
Sulphate of ammonia	*1.5 (3.3)*
Dried blood	*0.5 (1.1)*
Superphosphate	*2.0 (4.4)*
Bone meal	*0.5 (1.1)*
Sulphate of potash	*0.5 (1.1)*
Sulphate of iron	*0.5 (1.1)*

Weed control

Carefully maintaining your lawn and using good quality grass will greatly improve its ability to fight off weeds. However, you will almost inevitably come across the odd one. They appear as broad-leaved weeds, such as clover, moss and weed grasses.

Weed control using lawn sand

Broad-leaved weeds and moss can be eradicated with lawn sand, which also contains a fertilizer that will stimulate the grass to recover quickly.

1 Measure the area of lawn affected to determine how much lawn sand is required and mark it out with pegs and string. Then scatter it evenly over the area. Irrigate if there is no rain during the first two days after application.

2 When the moss and weeds have turned brown, use a fan rake to remove the debris, but rake from the edges of the affected area into its centre to prevent any live weeds spreading. Collect up and dispose of the these dead weeds.

Watering and aerating

Weeds are particularly prevalent in areas that suffer from compaction and poor drainage. So, by dealing with these problems first you can help to minimize the spread of weeds. Usually, the spring flush of grass at the beginning of the season is soft, lush and quickly shows signs of stress in dry conditions; by growing the grass 'hard' or slowly, it is possible to induce a degree of drought tolerance into the lawn.

1 To harden the grass, stop mowing the lawn so frequently and raise the height of the cut, to help the grass to shade its own roots and keep the soil cooler, which in turn will reduce evaporation.

2 To ease compaction, jab the tines of a garden fork into the surface of the soil to a depth of 5 cm (2 in) to ensure the hard surface crust or dead matted grass has been thoroughly penetrated.

3 Lay out the garden hose pipe on the lawn and run the water at a very slow rate. Leave the water running like this for several hours. This is the most effective way to water the lawn as the water soaks slowly and deeply into the soil. Frequent light waterings can encourage shallow rooting which makes the grass very prone to drought.

Lawn Repairs

If a lawn is used regularly, a certain amount of wear and tear is inevitable; edges become ragged or trodden by walking too close to the lawn edge, and bare patches occur due to mower settings being too low or the removal of a mat-forming weed. Although these blemishes look unsightly, they are quite easy to repair and the lawn can recover its health and appearance remarkably quickly.

Repairing a damaged lawn edge

1 To repair small sections of lawn edge mark out a square around the damaged area with pegs and string, and, using the string as a guide, cut out a square of turf from behind the damaged edge using a half-moon edger.

2 Using a spade or turfing iron, cut horizontally under the turf to a depth of about 5 cm (2 in); this will sever the roots enabling the turf to be lifted up.

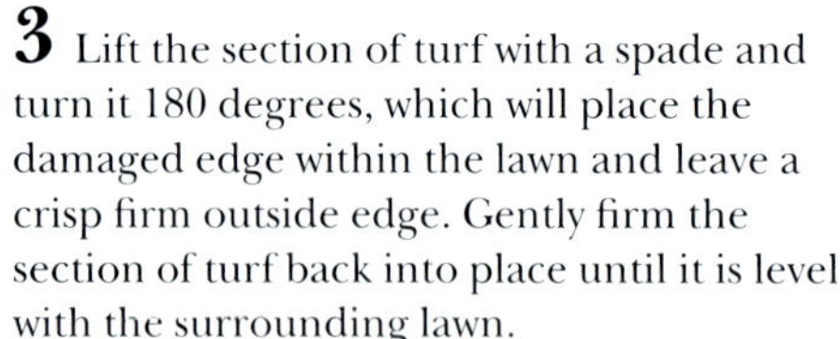

3 Lift the section of turf with a spade and turn it 180 degrees, which will place the damaged edge within the lawn and leave a crisp firm outside edge. Gently firm the section of turf back into place until it is level with the surrounding lawn.

4 The original damaged edge is filled with a sandy top dressing or garden soil and firmed until it is the same level as the lawn. Grass seed is then sown onto the top dressing and watered in. If the weather is dry, place a piece of loosely woven hessian sacking over the seeded area to prevent drying out and encourage rapid germination. Within 6 weeks the areas should have fully recovered.

Repairing a damaged patch

1 Using a fan rake, rake away all traces of old dead grass and debris to leave the patch of soil on the lawn bare.

2 Then use a hand fork to jab into the surface of the soil to a depth of about 2 cm (¾ in); this is to break up the surface and ease soil compaction.

3 Then using the fan rake again, rake the surface of the soil to a depth of about 2.5 cm (1 in) to create a fine tilth for a seed bed, ready to take the new grass seed.

4 Sow the grass seed evenly over the prepared area, at a rate equivalent to 30 g/sq m (1oz/sq yd) and immediately after sowing lightly rake the seed into the soil surface. A useful tip is to lay a piece of loosely woven hessian sacking over the seeded area to prevent drying out, encourage rapid germination, and deter birds from eating the seed.

Repairing humps and hollows

1 Using a half-moon edger, cut two lines into the lawn to form a cross, with the centre of the cross in the centre of the affected area. Make these cuts large enough so that they exceed the area to be levelled.

2 Using a spade or turfing iron, cut horizontally under the turf to a depth of about 5 cm (2 in). This will sever the roots enabling the turf to be lifted up. Cut from the centre of the cross out, into and under the lawn, as this causes less damage to the surface of the lawn.

3 Peel back the four sections of turf to expose the soil beneath; uncover a large area of soil as this will allow plenty of room to work within the affected lawn area.

4 For a hollow, fill the hollow beneath the turf with good quality topsoil and firm gently until it is level with the surrounding soil. For a hump, remove some soil until the hump is level with the surrounding soil.

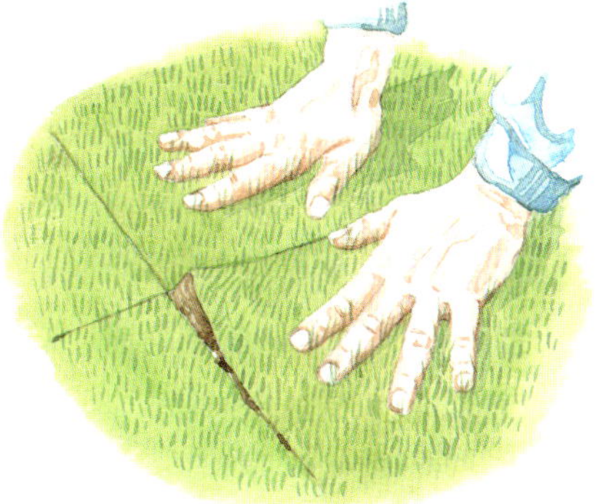

5 Finally, carefully replace the folded turf into its original position and firm gently until it is level with the surrounding lawn, or fractionally higher to allow for settling. Cover this area with a 1 cm (½ in) layer of sandy top dressing or sieved garden soil and then brush it into the joints to encourage them to re-establish their roots quickly.

Introducing Plants into Your Lawn

Though frequently undervalued as merely a flat green expanse which often requires a great deal of work, the lawn has an important contribution to make to the garden. A lawn is a basic feature of many gardens and can be purely functional, however, the addition of plants within the lawn area can make it a more colourful and highly ornamental feature.

Allium moly

Galanthus *'S. Arnott'*

Ornithogalum arabicum

Planting bulbs

Groups of bulbs can be planted beneath the turf in your lawn to introduce interest or lead the eye in a particular direction.

1 Use a half-moon edger to cut an 'H' shape in the turf. Cut under the turf with a spade or turfing iron and pull back the edges.

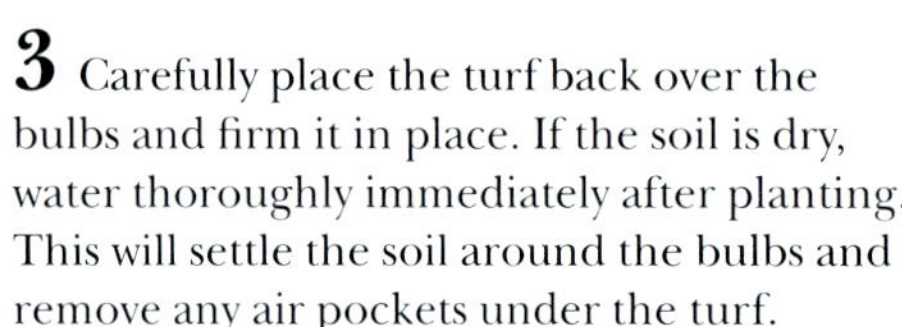

2 Loosen the soil and place the bulbs into the hole in an upright position, and press down into the soil. Then pull the soil back into the hole over the bulbs and firm in.

3 Carefully place the turf back over the bulbs and firm it in place. If the soil is dry, water thoroughly immediately after planting. This will settle the soil around the bulbs and remove any air pockets under the turf.

Suitable bulbs

Allium moly
Snowdrop (*Galanthus*)
Star-of-Bethlehem (*Ornithogalum*)

Planting trees and shrubs

A single tree or large shrub can be used to create an impressive focal point in a garden lawn. Be careful, however, in your selection of plant; some can cast too much shade and grass will not thrive. Trees such as birch (*Betula*) and honey locust (*Robinia*) are a good choice as they have a thin canopy and cast only a little shade over the grass.

1 With canes and string mark out a circle for the hole to at least twice the width of the plant's root system.

2 Remove the turf with a spade and stack it away from the working area.

3 Dig a hole which is at least twice the width of the plant's root system and deep enough to accommodate all of the roots.

4 Using a garden fork, break up the soil around the sides of the hole ,and in the bottom to a depth of at least 15 cm (6 in). This will reduce impaction and so will allow the new roots to spread into the soil surrounding the planting hole, allowing the plant to become established more quickly.

5 Carefully loosen some of the outermost roots on the root ball and then, taking the plant by its stem, gently place it in the prepared hole. Make sure it is positioned centrally with the root ball on the bottom, and use a bamboo cane to check that the plant is level with the surrounding soil.

6 Start to back-fill the hole with the soil that was removed, spreading it evenly around the roots. Shake the stem of the tree to settle the soil between the roots. This will also remove any air pockets around the roots.

7 Continue filling the hole with layers of soil, periodically shaking the tree stem, and firm each layer with your boot heel until the hole has been filled to its original level.

8 Apply a top dressing of fertilizer to the soil around the plant and mix this into the top 5 cm (2 in). This will gradually be washed down into the root zone.

herb walkway

The use of herbs was very popular in medieval England for carpeting green walkways. Chamomile was widely used, as was thyme, which has the added quality of being covered in a carpet of pinkish-purple flowers in the summer, as well as having a wonderfully aromatic smell. Growing a whole lawn can be expensive and time consuming as you would need hundreds of plants to create an instant display, so creating walkways around the garden is a much simpler method of introducing small stretches of these attractive plants.

materials & equipment

organic matter

general-purpose fertilizer

trowel, garden fork and rake

suitable herbs (see table opposite)

watering can

shears

routine care

Spring is an exciting time in the garden with the introduction of new plants and garden features, as well as being a period of rapid growth for new and established plants. However, in order to maintain a healthy and attractive garden, there are a number of routine tasks that must be attended to. These include feeding and watering and checking weed growth. The beginning of the season, when the work load is still light, is also the ideal time for attending to the basic maintenance of your garden buildings and structures and for checking that garden tools and machinery are in good working order. You may also need to install protective coverings for new plants to give them a better chance to establish themselves.

Feeding Plants

In order to grow well, plants need a balanced supply of nutrients, which they take up from the surrounding soil in a solution of water, using their roots. The nutrient reserves in the soil will eventually be depleted by the growing plants, however, unless they are replaced – an operation referred to as 'feeding' plants.

Fertilizers

Organic fertilizers

These consist of processed dead plant or animal matter, such as bone meal, dried blood and fish meal. They have a lower nutritional value than inorganic ones.

Inorganic fertilizers

These are derived from mineral deposits or manufactured by an industrial process and can be mixed to form a compound fertilizer. They are faster acting than organic fertilizers.

How to feed plants

Fertilizers are sold either in a dry, solid form as granules, pellets or powders, or as a liquid concentrate. They should be prepared and applied according to the instructions on the carton, because overfeeding can damage or even kill the plants. In general terms, liquid feeds are faster acting than dry ones and are usually used to correct nutrient deficiencies.

Applying dry fertilizer

1 If the soil is dry you will need to water it thoroughly before feeding. Mark out large areas to be treated into sections, calculate the amount of fertilizer required to treat each section, and sprinkle it evenly by hand. For individual plants simply scatter the powder or granules around the base of the plant to be treated.

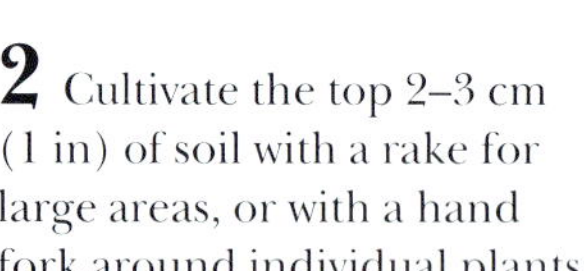

2 Cultivate the top 2–3 cm (1 in) of soil with a rake for large areas, or with a hand fork around individual plants to incorporate the fertilizer into the soil. Water the area to dissolve and wash down the fertilizer into the roots.

Applying liquid fertilizer

1 Liquid fertilizers must be diluted with water according to the manufacturer's instrctions. They are applied either with a watering can or hosepipe directly to the soil around the base of the plant.

2 Alternatively, they can be applied as a foliar feed, sprayed directly onto the foliage. Most foliar feeds are also soil-acting so that any fertilizer running off the leaves onto the soil can be absorbed by the roots.

Common nutrient deficiencies

	Symptoms	Causes	Susceptible plants	Control
Calcium	Overall reduction in growth, stunted shoot-tip growth, pale margin to the leaves, retarded root development.	Very low or very high soil pH, applying too much potassium and high rainfall.	Most plants, but especially apples and tomatoes (fruit is damaged).	Apply calcium nitrate.
Iron	Pale yellow leaves, stunted shoot-tips and an overall reduction in growth.	High pH and watering with tap water in 'hard water' areas.	Acid loving plants, including *Pieris*, *Camellia*, rhododendrons and heathers.	Apply acid mulches, incorporate suphur into the soil or apply trace elements or
Magnesium	Yellow blotches between the veins on the lower (older) leaves.	Oils with low pH leaching from poor, freely draining soils and loamless composts with high levels of potassium.	Fruiting plants, especially tomatoes.	Apply Epsom salts as a liquid feed or as a foliar feed.
Manganese	Yellowing of the leaves.	Soil pH of 7.0 or more.	Apples, peaches, peas and tomatoes.	Apply fertilizer containing manganese sulphate.
Nitrogen	Dull yellow leaves, thin spindly stems and overall reduction in growth.	Leaching from poor, freely-draining soils and loamless composts.	Any plants.	Apply high-nitrogen fertilizer, such as nitrochalk or sulphate of ammonia.
Phosphate	Young foliage is a dull bluish-green, later turning yellow.	Low pH and high rainfall; heavy clay soils locking up the content of phosphates.	Potentially any plant, particularly seedlings.	Apply phosphate or triple super-phosphate.
Potassium	Foliage turns bluish-purple, later changing to yellow with brown, dead margins and tips to the leaves; reduced growth; and poor flowering and fruit.	Growing plants in light or peaty soils, or soils that have a high pH.	Apples, blackcurrants and pears.	Apply sulphate of potash.

Malus *'Golden Hornet'*

Pieris japonica *'Geisha'*

Rhododendron narcissiforum

Watering

Some plants consist of up to 90 per cent water, which is constantly moving around within them and being lost from pores in the leaves as transpiration. Lost water must be replaced immediately so that the cells remain filled, in order to keep them firm and maintain the plant's structure. Water is therefore essential for encouraging rapid growth.

When to water

Choosing the correct time of day to water your garden can save on the amount of water lost to evaporation from the soil's surface. The soil is cooler and the atmosphere relatively moist in the early morning and late evening, so applying the water at those times will allow it the maximum time to soak in and be of most use to the growing plants.

Effective watering

1 Water needs to be delivered directly to the roots of the plant, or as close to the roots as possible. Seep- or trickle-irrigation systems work best and will deliver the water to a very specific point with the low pressure and steady flow allowing the water to soak into the rooting zone rather than spreading on the soil surface and evaporating.

2 Another simple but very efficient way of keeping water in the right area to benefit the plant is to create a shallow, saucer-shaped depression around the base of each plant. This way any water which is applied into the depression is held in place until it can soak into the soil where the majority of the roots are situated.

Plant requirements

Plants where the fruit is eaten have two critical watering periods: when they flower (to aid pollination and fruit set), and after the fruit shows obvious signs of swelling.

Some plants are more at risk from dry conditions than others: these include seedlings and newly-transplanted trees, shrubs, bedding plants, vegetables, plants sited in dry positions or near well-established competition and those in containers, hanging baskets and window boxes.

Preventive measures

There are various measures which can be taken to reduce moisture loss from the soil. Shading plants with netting or fleece is an effective way of reducing water stress, or you can use shelter barriers or windbreaks where strong winds may dry out the plants.

Weed Control

Weeds compete directly with plants for light, nutrients and water. They can also act as hosts to pests and diseases which can spread onto the crops as the season progresses. It is essential that they are removed, therefore, and the most effective system for clearing weeds is usually an on-going combination of both cultural and chemical methods, especially where established perennial weeds are to be eliminated.

Cultural weed control

The simplest way to deal with weeds is to physically remove them, either by pulling or digging them out of the soil, or if they are small they can be hoed off at soil level. There are a number of tools available for different types of weed. See right from top to bottom: a patio weeder is very useful in narrow spaces; a daisy grubber will remove large weeds from the lawn; a Dutch hoe works best for shallow rooted weeds; and a draw hoe is the most effective tool for chopping up deeper rooted weeds.

Mulching

Most weeds are found in the uppermost 6 cm (2½ in) and they will usually only germinate when exposed to light. Mulching blocks out sunlight and prevents weed seed germination. Organic mulches provide the added bonus of improving the fertility of the soil, but inorganic mulches are more effective because they form a better weed barrier. However, inorganic materials look rather unsightly and in order to get the best of both worlds, this type of mulch is often covered with a thin layer of organic material to make it aesthetically pleasing.

Chemical weed control

There are a number of chemicals (also called 'herbicides') which can be used to deal with weed problems, and they are certainly the quickest and most effective method of controlling established perennial weeds. But you must use them with the utmost care to avoid harming ornamental and cropping plants and, most importantly, humans and pets. When any chemical is to be applied, always read the manufacturer's directions on the carton very carefully and follow any instructions for dilution exactly. Chemical weed killers are sprayed directly onto the weeds when they are in full growth, then, as they start to die, they can be pulled out, or in large areas it is easier to dig over the soil in order to bury the dead weeds. As the next flush of weed seedlings start to germinate, spray them with the chemical weed killer again and remove as before.

Chemical weed killers are best applied with a spray gun.

Protecting and Supporting Plants

In the spring, many plants will still need protection from frost damage or damage from birds and other pests, to help advance growth and encourage earlier cropping or flowering. As they grow, many tall plants will also need supporting to stop the stems from bending over, and spring is the ideal time to set up a support structure, ready for the plant as it emerges from the soil.

Protective structures

Cloches

Glass, rigid plastic and Perspex covers offer the most effective form of frost protection. They can be purchased ready-made and placed over the plants that need protection (see right). However, bear in mind that they tend to lose temperature rapidly in the late afternoon and evening.

Fleece

Loosely woven or spun materials are now readily available. They don't provide a great deal of warmth but do maintain steady temperatures, making them ideal for short-term protection in early spring.

Plastic film

This material is inexpensive and easy to use. However, the air around the plants gets very hot during the day and loses heat rapidly during the night. Use for short-term protection and to give plants an early boost.

Screening

The very changeable weather conditions in the spring mean that young plants can be very easily damaged by sun scorch, particularly through glass. Some method of screening from very bright sunlight may well be necessary and should be applied earlier rather than later, after the damage has occurred. For small greenhouses, shade netting or blinds made from split canes can be draped over the roof to filter the sun's rays, but they may interfere with the roof ventilators. If this is a problem, the glass can be painted or sprayed with a proprietary glasshouse shading paint, or with diluted white emulsion paint.

Making a protective structure

A simple netting, hessian or plastic casing, held in place with canes, will prevent wind and frost damage whilst still permitting air circulation and allowing the plants to breathe. When the weather improves it can easily be removed.

1 Insert bamboo canes (four is usually enough) into the soil around the plants to be protected, making sure that the canes are taller than the actual plants.

2 Wrap netting, plastic mesh or hessian around the sides of the bamboo frame and secure with string, tied around the top, bottom and middle of the casing.

Supporting plants

As the weather starts to improve, later on in the season, the rapid growth of new plants can often take the gardener by surprise. In order to maintain the stature of your plants it may be necessary to erect a support system to protect the weak new stems from wind and rain damage. There are several different methods that can be used to support plants, depending on the size and habit of the plant, as well as its stage of growth.

Ties

Whatever method you use, you will need ties to attach the stem to the support structure. Garden string or twine is strong enough for most jobs and will stand up to a certain amount of wet weather. Plastic-coated wire is the strongest form of tie and has the added advantage of being waterproof.

Single stakes

Bamboo stakes are most commonly used and are ideal for single stemmed annuals and perennials, however, as these will rot over time, you might prefer to invest in metal stakes, some of which have a loop at the top for slipping the stem through. Insert the stake into the ground and tie the stem of your plant to it in a figure of eight.

Ring supports

Clump-forming or multi-stemmed plants may need a larger structure, such as a ring or link stake. You can make your own by inserting rings of canes and running string around them to hold the stems in place.

Plants that need supporting

- African marigold (*Tagetes erecta*)
- *Aster*
- Bellflower (*Campanula*)
- *Centaurea*
- *Dahlia*
- Delphinium
- Hollyhock (*Alcea rosea*)
- Larkspur (*Consolida ambigua*)
- Peony (*Paeonia*)
- *Salpiglossis*
- Sunflower (*Helianthus*)
- *Thunbergia alata*
- Tickseed (*Coreopsis*)

Aster amellus

Helianthus

Paeonia officinalis

Repairs

Just as you take care of the plants in your garden, so must you regularly check and maintain all the equipment and the structures that play such an important part in the health and appearance of your garden. The beginning of spring is the ideal time to carry out repairs of garden tools in preparation for the coming growing season.

Greenhouse repairs

If any sheets of glass are broken they should be replaced immediately, because without attention, in addition to the loss of heat, the wind will enter through the hole, causing more damage to the glass and the plants inside.

Aluminium alloy greenhouses
Remove the sprung metal clips which hold the glass in place, and take out the cracked or broken glass. Replace it with greenhouse or horticultural glass and return the metal slips.

Wooden greenhouses
With most wooden structures, the glass is held in place by a combination of a layer of putty onto which the glass is pressed, and small glazing nails called 'sprigs'; these hold the glass to the wooden glazing bars.

1 Start by removing the old glazing sprigs with a pair of pliers, and carefully take out any broken sections of glass which remain. Then chop out any old dry putty with a hammer and glazing knife or chisel.

2 Spread an even layer of soft putty over the area where the old putty was removed from the glazing bars. Slide the new sheet of glass into place and carefully press it onto the bed of putty. Care must be taken to apply pressure to the glass evenly or the sheet of glass will crack. Using a damp knife, remove any surplus putty from the glass and glazing bar.

3 Fix the sheet of glass into position by knocking the new sprigs into the glazing bars. When the glass is secured, it can be cleaned with a damp cloth.

Timber maintenance

Preserving wood
Wooden gates, fence posts and other wooden garden structures will require regular applications of a suitable wood preservative to prolong the life of the wood and guard against extreme weather conditions, such as rain and sun scorch.

1 Remove any surface mould or lichen with a wire-bristled brush and make sure that the wood is dry before painting begins – this is to ensure that the material will soak deeply into the wood for maximum protection.

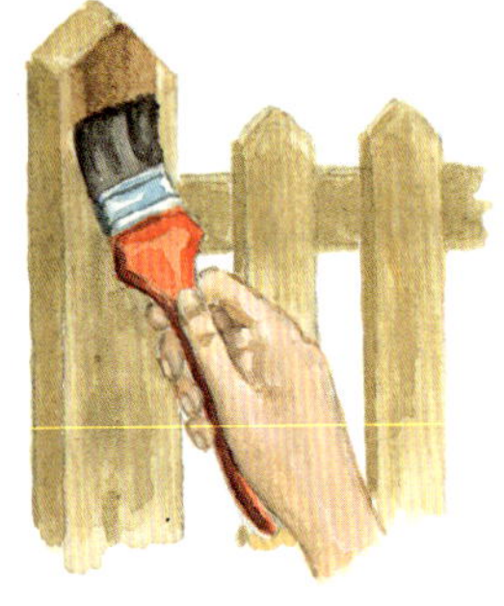

2 Apply the preservative with an old paint brush or garden sprayer, and take great care to protect any nearby plants by pulling them well away from the structure and covering them with polythene sheeting before any painting begins. It may be necessary to consider applying a second coat for sections close to ground level or where the end grain of the wood is exposed.

Repairing a rotten fence post

1 Prise out the fixing nails holding the side panels into the post and ease the fence panels away from the post.

2 Dig around the base of the post until it is loose and lever it out of the ground. Then saw through as much of the post as necessary to remove all traces of rotten wood.

3 Refill the hole and compact the soil to make it as firm as possible, leaving the surface level. Then hammer the new fence spike into the soil.

4 Set the repaired wooden post into the 'cup' in the top of the spike and fix the post into position so that it is steady and secure in the ground. Replace the side panels of the fence by pushing them back into line with the post. Use a spirit level as you do this to check that the top of each of the panels is still horizontal. Finally, fix them to the wooden post by nailing them into their original positions.

Garden tools

Early spring is a good time to thoroughly check over all gardening tools and equipment, as poorly maintained equipment tends to be ineffective and can damage plants by making ragged cuts and may also be a danger to the gardener.

Cutting tools

Clean knives, loppers and secateurs with vinegar to remove any dried sap and dirt from the blades. Then wash them with water to remove all traces of vinegar and dry them. Finally, wipe the metal parts of the tools with an oily cloth to prevent rusting (see below).

The blades should be run through a sharpener; this will need to be done throughout the growing season if they are to maintain their effectiveness.

Cultivating tools

These can be cleaned with an oily rag, (see left) and any splits or splinters in the handles should be smoothed over by rubbing them down with sandpaper.

making a decorative path

One of the best materials for creating a path is concrete, which is both durable and easy to install. To make it more interesting, bed other materials into the surface so that it is more pleasing to the eye, while still retaining its strength. One material that is often used in this way is pebbles, and for a chequerboard effect, strips of wood can be bedded into the concrete at regular intervals.

materials & equipment

pegs and string

spade, rake and garden roller

wooden retaining pegs 5 x 2.5 cm (2 x 1 in) and retaining boards

galvanized nails, 7.5 cm (3 in) long and spirit level

hardcore or rubble and sand

strips of wood 5 cm (2 in) wide and 10 cm (4 in) deep, enough for the sides and the chequerboard effect and saw and hammer

concrete (see step 8 opposite) and wheelbarrow

pebbles, about 7.5–10 cm (3–4 in) in diameter

stiff-bristled brush and polythene sheets

creating a raised bed

A raised planter provides a neat, clearly defined growing area where it is possible to work without having to stoop or bend too much. The height and shape add an extra dimension to the garden and a new growing surface. The soil or compost used can be of a different type to the surrounding soil, allowing, for example, acid loving plants, such as rhododendrons, to be grown even when the surrounding soil is alkaline. Plants which like a dry or free-draining site, such as alpines, also do very well in this slightly elevated growing environment.

materials & equipment

pegs and string

hand fork or garden fork

railway sleepers – not treated with wood preservative toxic to plants, or heavy wooden beams or logs of uniform size and thickness

galvanized nails, 15 cm (6 in) long and hammer

old carpet or turves

compost to suit chosen plants

plants of your choice to suit the soil

pond care

*The pond calendar year really begins in spring. As the water temperature rises, fish become more active and visible and the frogs come out of hibernation to begin breeding. Plants, such as the white marsh marigold (*Caltha palustris *var.* alba*) come into flower, followed by the yellow marsh marigold (*Caltha palustris*) which will flower until the end of the season. Many plants are also propagated at this time by cuttings, seed or division. If you do not have a pond in your garden, then early spring, when the soil is quite dry and firm, is the best time to start the construction of a new water feature. For existing ponds, general maintenance needs to be carried out now, but provided it is carried out on a regular basis this amounts to little work.*

Pond Maintenance

General maintenance is fairly minimal if carried out regularly and the pond need not be emptied every year, unless it has been neglected. After a number of years, however, silt and debris will gradually accumulate on the floor of the pond, which may lead to pollution, causing both the plants and the fish to suffer. Leaks may also occur as a result of frost damage, ground subsidence or even deterioration through age, and these must be repaired as soon as they are spotted.

Pond cleaning

When a thorough clean is required, choose a mild day in late spring, when the water is clear and it is easy to see the plants and fish in the pond. Temporary storage for the plants and fish can include barrels, buckets, or even large plastic bags.

1 Store any fish which are taken from the pond in containers, and keep them in water consisting of half clean water and half pond water, to help prevent the fish suffering from shock or stress.

2 Remove as many of the plants as possible before lowering the water level, taking out the marginal plants first, the deep water aquatics when some of the water has been drained away, and the floaters and oxygenators when they are within reach.

3 Completely drain the pond of water. To do this, use an electric pump, bail out or siphon off the water.

4 Then remove all silt and debris from the floor of the pond and scrub the walls with a stiff-bristled brush, regularly dipping it in clean water, but take care not to damage the lining of the pond.

5 After the pond has been cleaned, allow the sides to dry for a few hours, to kill off any pest and disease residue which may have escaped the cleaning process. Refill the pond with slow-running water.

6 Add the plants to be submerged by lowering them gently into the water when it is almost up to the required level, adding the marginals and floating plants last, once the water is starting to clear. Do not introduce the fish until the water is almost clear, as they may suffocate due to the particles in the cloudy water clogging their gills.

Spotting and repairing a leak

If the water level in your pond falls, do not automatically assume that it has a leak as this may be due to surface evaporation, especially in hot or windy weather. A constant drop in water level during cool, still weather is usually the first indicator that your pond has a leak, and one of the most common causes of damage to the pond liner is frost damage, which usually shows up in the spring. Allow the water level to fall and stabilize, as this will indicate the level of the damaged area. The first stage is to empy the pond: follow steps 1 to 3 as for 'Pond Cleaning', then brush away any dirt or weed residue and allow to dry.

Repairing flexible liners

1 Cut a patch from a liner repair sheet at least twice as long and twice as wide as the damaged area, and clean the patch and the damaged area with methylated spirits (to ensure a good adhesion).

2 Apply a liberal covering of special waterproof bonding cement or a strip of double-sided adhesive to both the patch and the damaged area of the liner.

3 When the adhesive feels 'tacky', place the patch over the damaged area and smooth down to ensure a good bonding and remove any air bubbles. Check the repair after 24 hours, and if it is firmly bonded to the liner, refill the pond (see steps 5 and 6 in 'Pond Cleaning' opposite).

Concrete liner

1 Using a hammer and mason's chisel, gently chisel out some of the concrete around the crack to make it a little wider than the original damaged section – this will help to strengthen the final repair.

2 Brush out all loose dirt and debris from the crack and carefully fill the crack with a special waterproof mastic cement.

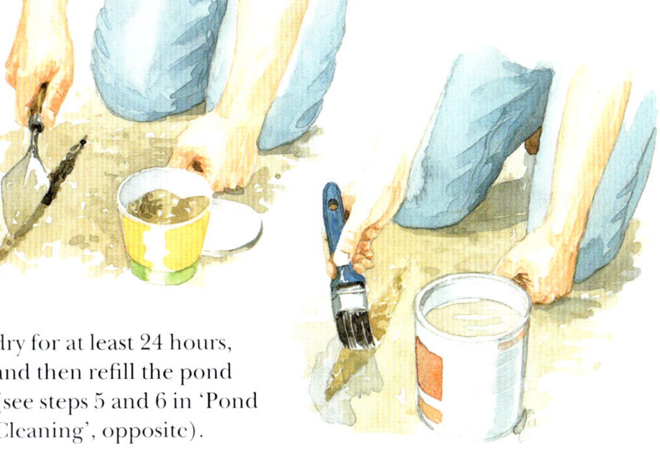

3 Once the cement is dry, paint the lining with two or three coats of waterproof pond sealant. Leave this to dry for at least 24 hours, and then refill the pond (see steps 5 and 6 in 'Pond Cleaning', opposite).

Introducing New Plants

Aquatic plants should be moved or transplanted while they are actively growing as they re-establish better if moved during the growing season. The best time to move them is in the late spring, as this will give them the maximum period of time to establish themselves in their new surroundings before the onset of winter.

Planting aquatics

Most aquatics are planted and grown in submerged basket-like containers, the advantages being that it gives the gardener a greater degree of control over the growing environment and makes the plants more accessible for inspection and propagation. The usual material used for containers is heavy-gauge rigid plastic – wood and metal containers should be avoided because they may produce toxins harmful to fish.

If you are planting water lilies, trim any rotting or dead sections of rootstock and any damaged leaves before planting.

1 Line the mesh container with sacking or heavy-gauge paper, to stop the compost spilling out through the mesh.

2 Half-fill the lined basket with compost and then use scissors to trim off any surplus paper or sacking around the outside of the container.

3 Place the plant firmly into the centre of the basket, taking care to hold it by its stem, not by the roots. Add more compost and pack it around the plant so that is is held firmly in position.

4 Fill the basket until the compost is 2–3 cm (1 in) from the rim. To anchor the compost when the bucket is submerged, top up with a 1 cm (½ in) layer of gravel over the compost.

5 Water the container thoroughly to soak the plant and help settle the compost around the roots.

6 To lower the basket into the pond, it is a good idea to attach string handles to the sides of the basket, so you do not have to drop it in position.

Propagation

The method of propagation most commonly used for marginals and deep-water aquatics, as well as for bog plants, is taking cuttings. Oxygenators, deep-water aquatics and some marginals, particularly those with thicker roots, are best propagated by division. Floaters, on the other hand, can be propagated very simply from offsets.

Cuttings

1 Take your cuttings in late spring when the shoots are about 10–12.5 cm (4–5 in) long. Select non-flowering shoots, remove the lower leaves and trim them to just below a leaf joint (node) to produce a cutting about 7–8 cm (3 in) long.

2 The cuttings can be planted singly or arranged in bunches of six to eight cuttings, tied together at the base with string.

3 Plant the clump or stem into a basket mesh container suitable for a pond. Fill it with loam-based compost up to the rim and make a planting hole. Insert the plants and firm the compost around them. Then stand the base of the basket in a saucer or tray of water to keep the compost permanently wet and place the cuttings in a cool, partially shaded position. Establish them in the pond in 2 or 3 weeks time once roots have formed.

Division

1 Lift the plant to be divided from the pond, complete with its container, then gently tip it out of its container. For bog plants, simply lift the plant from the soil with a hand fork.

2 Wash the plant thoroughly to make sure all of it is clearly visible. Inspect the plant and remove any rotting or diseased sections and discard any old or weak stems and shoots.

3 Divide the roots into sections, keeping the young, healthy divisions in a bucket of water to prevent them drying out. Replant the divisions into containers (see opposite).

Offsets

For floating aquatic plants, the process of propogation is remarkably simple. Lift the individual plants out of the water, then carefully break off the young healthy pieces of plant that you wish to keep, and place them back in the pond to grow into larger plants. Any old sections of plant that you do not need can simply be discarded.

Care of Established Plants

The plants growing in and around the pond will require annual maintenance in the spring. As the season progresses, the water in the pond will slowly rise in temperature, encouraging aquatic plants and marginals to show the first visible signs of growth. However, this is a time for extreme caution, with the weather and air temperature in particular being very changeable.

Spring tasks

Once established, most pond plants require little attention. Watch out for frost damage at the beginning of the season, however, when the shoot tips and flowers are scorched by low temperatures or cold winds. Remove any discoloured or withered leaves to encourage the plant to recover – this is important as any plant debris allowed to accumulate in the water can lead to a shortage of oxygen, which will be harmful to the fish.

Different types of pond plants have different functions in maintaining the natural balance within the pond. Check that your plants are in the right positions and numbers to suit the pond size and environment.

Bog plants

These plants love a rich, peaty, damp soil and they grow best with cool, damp roots close to water. Most of these plants are herbaceous perennials and will need lifting and dividing every 3 years or so (see page 97). Grow them close to the pond's edge where they provide shade for the young fish to congregate.

Primula sibirica

Bog plants

Anemone rivularis
Cardamine pratensis
Hosta
Iris ensata
Lobelia cardinalis
Primula alpicola

Deep-water aquatics

These plants are planted in containers and placed in the bottom of the pond – it is a good idea to cover them with a top dressing of gravel to help weigh them down. They will grow up from a depth of 45–60 cm (1½–2ft) and their leaves stretch up and float on the surface. They are useful for providing shelter for the fish as well as a place for them to spawn. Also, the leaves help to keep the water clear as they deprive food and light from the algae. Some of these plants will grow quite happily in moving water, so can be submerged near a fountain or water course; others are particularly well suited to conditions of partial shade or deep water.

Deep-water aquatics

Aponogeton distachyos
Euryale ferox
Nuphar advena
Nymphoides indica
Orontium aquaticum

Floaters

These plants provide a decorative cover on the surface of the pond, as they float with the leaves and stems above the water with their trailing roots submerged. There are two basic types: the larger-leaved types, such as water chestnut (*Trapa natans*), and the much smaller-leaved floaters which include ivy-leaved duckweed (*Wolffia*) and fairy moss (*Azolla caroliniana*). The smaller-leaved floaters tend to be very invasive and in warm, damp conditions these plants can increase rapidly and almost take over the surface of the pond, especially in warm damp spring conditions, so keep them in check, removing any excessive growth.

Floaters

Azolla caroliniana
Eichhornia crassipes
Hydrocharis morsus-ranae
Lemna trisulca
Stratiotes aloides
Trapa natans
Utricularia vulgaris
Wolffia

Marginals

Purely decorative, this group of plants do not really contribute to the ecological balance of the pond in the way that other groups of plants do. Most will grow well in a depth of 15–30 cm (6–12 in) of water. Marginals growing close to the pond do better if they are lifted and divided every third year just like most other herbaceous perennials.

Caltha palustrus

Marginals

Acorus gramineus
Caltha leptosepala
Decodon verticillatus
Iris laevigata
Mentha aquatica
Ranunculus lingua
Sparganium erectum
Thalia dealbata

Oxygenators

These plants have leaves which absorb carbon dioxide and minerals and despite their common name, these functions are far more important than producing oxygen and are very important for the clarity and quality of the pond water. They should be fully submerged with only the flowers on or above the surface of the water. Plant them in soil-filled containers, but keep different species separate to avoid competition. Oxygenators also provide perfect shelter for fish, as well as food. To create the right balance in the pond, there should be about three plants to each square metre (3 square feet) of pool.

Oxygenators

Callitriche hermaphroditica
Egeria densa
Fontinalis antipyretica
Mentha cervina
Myriophyllum aquaticum
Potamogeton crispus

Water lilies

This group consists of one genus (*Nymphaea*), with a submerged rootstock and roots up to 1.2 m (4 ft) deep, depending on the species. The leaves float on the surface and the flowers, that come in a wide range of colours, are held on or above the surface. They prefer full sun and still water and provide perfect shelter for the fish in the pond.

Nymphaea *'Froebelii'*

Water lilies

Blue lotus (*Nymphaea caerulae*)
Nymphaea 'Aurora'
Nymphaea tetragona
White water lily (*Nymphaea alba*)

Pond Weed

As light levels increase in the spring, not only do the ornamental plants begin to grow but so do the weeds. New ponds where the natural water balance is not yet fully established are particularly susceptible, but it is worth waiting for the pond to settle before taking any drastic action to remove the weeds. The introduction of healthy plants, including oxygenators, helps to starve weeds of necessary light and nutrients and should check their growth, however, you will almost certainly encounter some which appear to be increasing and will need to be eradicated.

Blanket weed

This is an algae which uses light and the nitrogen in the water to grow rapidly in mid spring. Thick layers of blanket weed can be effectively cleared by dragging it out on a stick or a garden rake. The weed may contain beneficial insects and water snails, so to avoid removing too many of these, leave the piles of blanket weed on the side of the pond overnight to give any creatures the chance to crawl back into the water. For more persistent cases of blanket weed, chemical controls are available.

An effective preventive measure is to float a hessian sack of straw or hay in the pond in early spring. Another useful and easy trick is to stuff the hay into an old pair of tights, secured at the end with a knot, which can then be thrown into the pond. Nitrogen used by bacteria to attack the hay then deprives the blanket weed of the necessary nutrients to develop any further.

Duckweed

Duckweed is mainly found growing on still water. This weed is made up of small clusters of leaves with roots attached to them that hang into the water. It does have some beneficial effect – the fish really seem to enjoy eating it – but it quickly covers the surface of the pond, blocking out the light and killing or considerably weakening submerged plants. Drag it out with a fine gauge net or colander and always make sure that at least one-third of the water's surface area is kept free of duckweed.

Fish Care

If you already have fish established in your pond you will notice that they become more active in spring as their rate of metabolism increases. As they start to move around they will need to be fed liberally to build up their strength, which will also help to protect them from diseases, which are more prevalent in this season. With new ponds, now is the time to introduce your fish to their new home, once the severe weather has passed.

Looking after your fish

In an established pond, regular feeding of the fish in spring and summer may not always be necessary, due to the insect population living in and around the pond.

Watch the movement of the fish to monitor any change in their behaviour. The usual signs of potential problems are either slow and sluggish behaviour from individual fish, while others remain active, or frenzied swimming, frequent surfacing and body rubbing against the side of the pond. If a problem is suspected it is a good idea to have a closer look at them; lift them with a net and place them in a separate container for examination so that the correct treatment can then be administered.

Make sure you do not over-feed the fish in the pond as this can be harmful, especially in a small pond where uneaten food decomposes and pollutes the water.

Introducing new fish

An average initial stocking rate is ten fish to every square metre (3 square feet) of pond surface. Hardy fish which can live together include goldfish, golden orfe, rudd, tench and shubunkins. Golden orfe and rudd should be introduced in quantity as they naturally prefer to swim in shoals. Tench are shy and prefer to live at the bottom of the pond, scavenging on insect larvae.

New fish are usually transported in polythene bags part-filled with water and inflated with oxygen. Ideally, the pond should have been planted at least a month before the fish are introduced to allow the plants to develop new roots and establish sufficiently to start producing new growth. It takes this amount of time to establish an ecological balance within the pond.

1 Place the container holding the fish on the surface of the pond to allow the water in the pond and the container to reach the same temperature. This will prevent the fish suffering temperature shock when they are released.

2 After 2 to 3 hours you can open the container and tip the fish into their new environment. Tilt it into the pond water, allowing the fish to adjust and swim slowly into the pond. After an hour, scatter some food over the surface of the pond.

making a small pond

In many respects the basic question about making a pond is a simple one – how to make a hole in the ground which will hold water for long periods of time. The solution is to line the hole with some form of waterproof material and in this respect there is a wealth of choice, including concrete, flexible and semi-rigid liners and moulded pre-formed liners. Flexible liners are the most satisfactory solution as they can be moulded into any shape. They are also the most economical method of lining a pond, as well as being the lightest for handling.

materials & equipment

length of hose or rope

spade

plank and spirit level

old carpet or fibreglass insulation material to fit hole

synthetic rubber or plastic lining sheet to fit hole

slabs or bricks for edge

mortar

pond plants (see opposite)

Glossary

Aerate
To loosen by physical or mechanical means to allow the penetration of air.

Algae
Primitive green plants which form a scum-like layer in ponds.

Alpine
A plant originating in mountainous regions, often applied to rock garden plants.

Annual
A plant which completes its reproduction cycle in one year.

Aquatic
Any plant which grows in water (may be anchored or free floating).

Bare-root
Plants with no soil on their roots (usually grown in the field and dug up for sale).

Base dressing
An application of fertilizer or organic matter incorporated into the soil.

Bedding plants
Plants arranged in mass displays (beds) to form a colourful temporary display.

Bed system
A system of growing vegetables in closely spaced rows to form blocks of plants.

Biennial
A plant which completes its life cycle in two growing seasons.

Bleeding
The excessive flow of sap, usually from spring pruned plants.

Bog plant
A plant which prefers to grow in damp soil conditions.

Bolt
The premature flowering and seed production of a cropping plant.

Brassica
Belonging to the cabbage family.

Broadcasting
The technique of spreading fertilizer or seeds randomly.

Bud
A condensed shoot containing an embryonic shoot or flower.

Compost
A potting media made to a standard formula; loam- or peat-based. Also well-rotted organic matter, such as garden waste.

Coppicing
The severe pruning of plants to ground level on an annual basis.

Crop rotation
A system of moving crops in a planned cycle to improve growth and help control pests and diseases.

Cultivar
A plant form which originated in cultivation rather than from the wild.

Cutting
A portion of a plant used for propagation.

Dead-heading
The deliberate removal of dead flower heads.

Deciduous
Plants which produce new leaves in the spring and shed them in the autumn.

Dormancy
A period of reduced growth, usually from late autumn through the winter.

Drill
A narrow straight line made in the soil for sowing seeds into.

Earthing up
A process of mounding up the soil around the base of a plant.

Evergreen
Plants which retain their actively growing leaves through the winter.

Fertile
A soil, rich in nutrients and biological life.

Fruit
The seed bearing vessel on a plant.
Fungicide
A chemical used to control fungal disease.
Germination
The development of a seed into a plant.
Grafting
A propagation method involving the joining of two or more separate plants together.
Graft union
The point where a cultivar is grafted onto a rootstock.
Ground cover
The term used to describe low-growing plants.
Half hardy
A plant which can tolerate low temperatures but is killed by frost.
Hardy
A plant which can tolerate temperatures below freezing without protection.
Herbaceous
A non-woody plant with an annual top and a perennial root system or storage organ.
Herbicide
A chemical used to kill weeds.
Inorganic
A man-made chemical compound (one which does not contain carbon).
Insecticide
A chemical used to kill insects.
Irrigation
A general term used for the application of water to soil and plants.
Lateral
A side shoot arising from an axillary bud.
Layering
A propagation technique where roots are formed on a stem before it is detached from the parent plant.
Leaching
The loss of nutrients by washing them through the soil.
Leader
The main dominant shoot or stem of the plant (usually the terminal shoot).
Legume
A member of the pea family that bears seeds in pods.
Lime
An alkaline substance formed from calcium.
Loam
A soil with equal proportions of clay, sand and silt.
Marginal plant
A plant which prefers to grow in damp soil conditions or partially submerged in water.
Mulch
A layer of material applied to cover the soil.
Nutrients
The minerals (fertilizers) used to feed plants.
Organic
Materials derived from decomposed animal or plant remains.
Oxygenator
An aquatic plant which releases oxygen into the water.
Peat
Decayed mosses, rushes or sedges.
Perennial
A plant which has a life-cycle of three years or more.
Pesticide
A chemical used to control pests.
pH
The level of acidity or alkalinity in a soil, measured on a scale of 1 to 14; 7 is neutral, below 7 is acid, and above 7 is alkaline.
Pinching out
The removal (with finger and thumb) of the growing point of a plant to encourage the development of lateral shoots.
Pollarding
The severe pruning of the main branches of a tree or shrub to the main stem or trunk.
Propagation
Different techniques used to multiply a number of plants.
Rhizome
A specialized underground stem which lies horizontally in the soil.
Root ball
The combined root system and surrounding soil or compost of a plant. Plants are often sold in this form, wrapped in hessian.
Root pruning
The cutting of live plant roots to control the vigour of a plant.
Rootstock
The root system onto which a cultivar is budded or grafted.
Sap
The juice or blood of a plant.
Scion
The propagation material taken from a cultivar or variety which is to be used for budding or grafting.
Shrub
A woody stemmed plant.
Stooling
The severe pruning of plants to within 10–15 cm (4–6 in) of ground level on an annual basis.
Sucker
A shoot arising from below ground level.
Tender
A plant which is killed or damaged by low temperatures, usually –10°C (50°F).
Tilth
A fine crumbly layer of surface soil.
Tip prune
Cutting back the growing point of a shoot to encourage the development of lateral shoots.
Top dressing
An application of fertilizer or bulky organic matter added to the soil surface.
Vegetative growth
Non-flowering stem growth.

Useful Addresses

Nurseries and Garden Centres

Alexandra Palace Garden Centre
Alexandra Palace
London N22

Bressingham Plant Centre
Dorney Court
Dorney, Windsor
Berkshire SL4 6QP

Burncorse Nurseries
Gwennap Redruth
Cornwall
TR16 6BJ

Clifton Nursery
5a Clifton Villas
London W9 2PH

Cravens Nursery
1 Foulds Terrace
Bingley
West Yorkshire BK10 4LZ

Deacons Nursery
Moorview
Godshill
Isle of Wight

Highfield Nurseries
Whitminster
Gloucester
GL2 7PL

Hillier Nurseries
Ampfield House
Romsey, Hants
SO51 9PA

Kennedy's Garden Centres
Kennedy House
11 Crown Row
Bracknell
Berks
RG12 0TH

Notcutt's Garden Centre and Waterers Nursery
150 London Road
Bagshot
Surrey GU19 5DG

Scotts Nurseries
Merriott
Somerset TA16 5PL

The Chelsea Gardener
125 Sydney Street
London SW3

The Van Hage Garden Company
Great Amwell Nr Ware
Hertfordshire SG12 9RP

Wyevale Garden Centre
Oakley Road
Keston
Kent BR2 6BY

For Hedges, Trees, and Shrubs:

Beechcroft Nurseries
Dept PG Appleby
Cumbria, CA16 6UE

Crowders Nurseries
London Road
Horncastle
Lincs, LN9 5LZ

Ian Roger
RV Roger Ltd
The Nurseries
Pickering
N Yorks
YO18 7HG

Rolawn (Turf Growers) Ltd
Elvington
York
N Yorks
YO4 5AR

Weasdale Nurseries
Kirkby Stephen
Cumbria
CH7 4LX

For Clematis:

Bushey Fields Nursery
Herne
Herne Bay
Kent CT6 7LJ

For Roses:

Mattock's Roses
The Rose Nurseries
Nuneham Courtenay
Oxford OX44 9PY

David Austin Roses
Albrighton
Wolerhampton WV7 3HB

For Bulbs:

Avon Bulbs
Burnt House Farm
Mid Lambrook
South Petherton
Somerset
TA13 5HE

Jacque Amand Nurseries
Clamp Hill
Stanmore
Middlesex
HA7 3JS

Van Tubergen UK
Dept 723
Bressingham
Diss
Norfolk
IP22 2AB

Winchester Bulbs
Winnal Down Farm
Alresford Road
Winchester
Hants
SO21 1HF

For Seeds:
Basically Seeds
Risby Business Park
Risby
Bury St Edmunds
Suffolk
IP28 6RD

Mr Fothergill's Seeds
Gazeley Road
Kentford, Newmarket
Suffolk
CB8 7QB

Marshalls
SE Marshall & Co Ltd
Regal Road
Wisbech
Cambs
PE13 2RF

Suttons Seeds Ltd
Hele Road
Torquay
Devon
TQ2 7QL

Unwins Seeds Ltd
Freepost
3241
Cambs
CB4 422

For Trellis:
Stuart Garden Architecture
Burrow Hill Farm
Wiveliscombe
Somerset
TA4 2RN

For Polytunnels:
Ferryman Polytunnels
Dept PG, Bridge Road
Lapford, Crediton
Devon EX17 6AH

For Fleece:
Agralon Limited
The Old Brickyard
Ashton Keynes, Swindon
Wiltshire
SN6 6QR

Agriframes Ltd
Charlwoods Road
East Grinstead
Sussex
RH19 2HG

For Water Gardens:
Lotus Water Products
PO Box 36
Junction Street
Burnley
Lancashire
BB12 0NA

Stapeley Water Gardens
London Road
Stapely
Nantwich
Cheshire
CW5 7LH

Timber and Building Supplies

B & Q Warehouse
Beckton Triangle
London
E6
and nationwide

Sainsbury's Homebase
195 Warwick Road
London
W14 8PU
and nationwide

Harcros Timber & Building Supplies Ltd
Harcros House
1 Central Road
Worester Park
Surrey
KT4 8DN

Atco Qualcast
Stowmarket
Suffolk
IP14 1EY

Fertilizers and Mulches

Miracle Garden Care Ltd
Fernhurst
Haslemere
Surrey

Phostrogen Ltd
Corwen
Flintshire
Wales
LL21 0EE

William Sinclair Holdings
Firth Road
Lincoln
Lincs
LN6 7AH

Credits

l. = left, **c.** = centre, **r.** = right, **t.** = top, **b.** = bottom

The photographer, Anne Hyde, wishes to make the following acknowledgements: Peter Aldington, Garden Designer of Turn End, Haddenham, Bucks; Vivien and John savage, Stockgrove Park, Bucks; Mr and Mrs D. Ingall, Irthlingborough, Northants; Mr and Mrs Douglas Fuller, The Crossing House, Shepreth, Cambridge; Merle and Peter Williams, Ickleford, Herts; Glen and Beverley Williams, Ickleford, Herts; Mrs Easter, Harpenden, Herts; Mr Siggers, Wichert, Ford, Bucks.

All photographs taken by Anne Hyde except for the following: p. 18 **b.**, p. 68 **l.**, **c.**, **r.**, p. 77 **l.**, **c.**, **r.**, p. 81 **l.**, **c.**, **r.**, p. 98, p. 99 **t.**, **b.** Jerry Harpur

Also thanks to the Principal at Capel Manor Horticulture Centre, Bullsmoor Lane, Enfield and the Editor of Gardening Which, PO Box 44, Hertford X, SG14 1SH.

Index

Page numbers in italics refer to illustrations.

Jacque Amand Nurseries
Clamp Hill
Stanmore
Middlesex
HA7 3JS

Van Tubergen UK
Dept 723
Bressingham
Diss
Norfolk
IP22 2AB

Winchester Bulbs
Winnal Down Farm
Alresford Road
Winchester
Hants
SO21 1HF

For Seeds:

Basically Seeds
Risby Business Park
Risby
Bury St Edmunds
Suffolk
IP28 6RD

Mr Fothergill's Seeds
Gazeley Road
Kentford, Newmarket
Suffolk
CB8 7QB

Marshalls
SE Marshall & Co Ltd
Regal Road
Wisbech
Cambs
PE13 2RF

Suttons Seeds Ltd
Hele Road
Torquay
Devon
TQ2 7QL

Unwins Seeds Ltd
Freepost
3241
Cambs
CB4 422

For Trellis:

Stuart Garden Architecture
Burrow Hill Farm
Wiveliscombe
Somerset
TA4 2RN

For Polytunnels:

Ferryman Polytunnels
Dept PG, Bridge Road
Lapford, Crediton
Devon EX17 6AH

For Fleece:

Agralon Limited
The Old Brickyard
Ashton Keynes, Swindon
Wiltshire
SN6 6QR

Agriframes Ltd
Charlwoods Road
East Grinstead
Sussex
RH19 2HG

For Water Gardens:

Lotus Water Products
PO Box 36
Junction Street
Burnley
Lancashire
BB12 0NA

Stapeley Water Gardens
London Road
Stapely
Nantwich
Cheshire
CW5 7LH

Timber and Building Supplies

B & Q Warehouse
Beckton Triangle
London
E6
and nationwide

Sainsbury's Homebase
195 Warwick Road
London
W14 8PU
and nationwide

Harcros Timber & Building Supplies Ltd
Harcros House
1 Central Road
Worester Park
Surrey
KT4 8DN

Atco Qualcast
Stowmarket
Suffolk
IP14 1EY

Fertilizers and Mulches

Miracle Garden Care Ltd
Fernhurst
Haslemere
Surrey

Phostrogen Ltd
Corwen
Flintshire
Wales
LL21 0EE

William Sinclair Holdings
Firth Road
Lincoln
Lincs
LN6 7AH

Credits

l. = left, **c.** = centre, **r.** = right, **t.** = top, **b.** = bottom

The photographer, Anne Hyde, wishes to make the following acknowledgements: Peter Aldington, Garden Designer of Turn End, Haddenham, Bucks; Vivien and John savage, Stockgrove Park, Bucks; Mr and Mrs D. Ingall, Irthlingborough, Northants; Mr and Mrs Douglas Fuller, The Crossing House, Shepreth, Cambridge; Merle and Peter Williams, Ickleford, Herts; Glen and Beverley Williams, Ickleford, Herts; Mrs Easter, Harpenden, Herts; Mr Siggers, Wichert, Ford, Bucks.

All photographs taken by Anne Hyde except for the following: p. 18 **b.**, p. 68 **l.**, **c.**, **r.**, p. 77 **l.**, **c.**, **r.**, p. 81 **l.**, **c.**, **r.**, p. 98, p. 99 **t.**, **b.** Jerry Harpur

Also thanks to the Principal at Capel Manor Horticulture Centre, Bullsmoor Lane, Enfield and the Editor of Gardening Which, PO Box 44, Hertford X, SG14 1SH.

Index

Acknowledgements

In putting the book together, I am most grateful to Toria Leitch and Caroline Davison for working my fingers to the bone, and my wife Val Bradley for proof reading my text (who thought my grammar was laughable). I would also like to thank Anne Hyde for her excellent photographs and Ashley Western and Prue Bucknall for their design input.